Guitar Terms for BEGINNERS A-Z

Tiff Bryan

www.YOURGUITARBRAIN.com

Want free goodies?

Email us at

info@yourguitarbrain.com

Title the email subject
"Goodies Guitar Terms A-Z"
tell us which term you liked learning
best, and we'll send some cool
stuff your way!

If you have a question, shoot us an email anytime!
info@yourguitarbrain.com

Love to play your guitar better?

Check out more of our books that'll help you save time and feel confident on guitar by scanning the QR code below!

Or visit

↓

https://geni.us/YourGuitarBrainAmazon

QR Code Instructions:

- Open your phone's camera app
- Point at the QR code (camera will auto recognise)
- Follow on-screen instructions; tap to open in browser
- Go to Amazon!

Contents

PART THREE 119

Guitar & Music Slang Terms 120

Slang for Guitar Sounds 121

Introduction

What does "guitar action" mean, and how can it make your guitar playing smoother and easier? What are "arpeggios", how can they improve your finger strength *and* take your creativity to the next level? And what on Earth is a "jazz box"? Find all the answers, and more, in this essential music terms reference guide.

Hey, fellow guitar player! **If you want to play great guitar, you need to know more than just notes and chords – you need to know the words**. It's true. And knowing the terms will help you improve your grasp of the guitar *and* the music you're playing. Win-Win!

Guitar Terms for Beginners A-Z helps you learn all the common guitar and music words and phrases and what they mean. A must-have for any guitarist, from beginner to experienced, **this book is your ultimate no-fuss A-Z glossary of guitar definitions**.

Broken down in an easily accessible way – no matter how long you've been playing the guitar – prepare yourself to say bye-bye to confusion and avoid feeling like a newbie nitwit.

This Book Will Help You

- Get all the correct information you need from a single reliable place – no more shaky online sources
- Feel more confident to call yourself a guitarist
- Feel inspired to try exciting new playing techniques
- Feel motivated to explore new music styles
- Feel confident to talk with other musicians
- Follow guitar tutorials easier
- Feel more knowledgeable about gear and effects
- Feel a sense of fulfilment from your new know-how

Terms You'll Learn

- **Playing Techniques** (e.g. Alternate Picking & Slurs)
- **Basic Music Theory** (e.g. Interval & Key Signature)
- **Rhythm** (e.g. Beats & Note Values)
- **Fun Guitar Slang** (e.g. "Gitfiddle" & "Chops")
- **Guitar Parts** (e.g. Pickups & Whammy Bar)
- **Guitar Maintenance** (e.g. Action & Setup)
- **Scales & Chords** (e.g. Triad & Pentatonic Scale)
- **Music Genres** (e.g. Blues, Bebop & Rockabilly)
- **Songwriting** (e.g. Song Parts & Arrangement)
- **Sounds & Effects** (e.g. Overdrive, Fuzz & FX Pedals)
- **Gear & Accessories** (e.g. Capo, Combo Amp & DAW)

You got this, superstar!

Tiff

About the Author

Tiff is a professional session guitarist with extensive experience in live performance, touring, T.V. work and recording studio sessions. She has worked with top-selling artists, such as Lady Gaga, Little Mix and Craig David. As a songwriter, Tiff has composed music for film, radio, and video games.

As a guitar tutor and mentor, with more than two decades' experience, Tiff is passionate about helping guitar players overcome bad habits to achieve more progress in a few months than they would in a lifetime.

Through her website, **YourGuitarBrain.com**, Tiff provides a valuable resource for inspiration, skill improvement, and frustration-free guitar learning.

N.B. The author wishes to say a heartfelt thank you to her guitar student Mark for the initial spark of inspiration from which this book came.

How to Use This Book

Use the book to look up any unfamiliar guitar-related terms you come across while reading instructional books, online forums or watching guitar videos.

You can quiz yourself or a friend on the terms and their meanings, and highlight any you're having trouble remembering.

Alphabetical Order

The phrases in this book are listed alphabetically to make them quick and easy to find. Look for the first letter of a word, expression or phrase you want to learn.

Bold Term Links

When you spot **bold** words or phrases in definitions, they're cross-references found in italics at the bottom, so you can quickly look them up in the book for more explanation (see Fig. 1.0.).

Category Brackets

Categories in square brackets next to term titles show which area of guitar playing or music the term typically belongs to. Terms with no category can be used in any area of music (see Fig. 1.0.).

The categories are:

[Music Theory] Terms usually related to essential basic need-to-know guitar music theory.

[Rhythm & Notation] Words and phrases associated with rhythm guitar and music notation.

[Playing Technique] Terms that refer to the skills you use to play melodies (e.g. riffs) and harmony (e.g. chords) on the guitar.

[Guitar Types] Terms that plunge into the world of guitar body shapes and help you learn about their unique features and differences so you know what to look for in your next guitar.

[Genre] See 'Music Genres' on the next page.

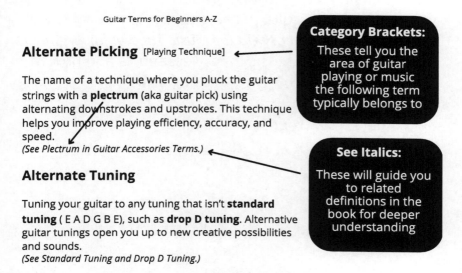

Guitar Terms for Beginners A-Z

Alternate Picking [Playing Technique]

The name of a technique where you pluck the guitar strings with a **plectrum** (aka guitar pick) using alternating downstrokes and upstrokes. This technique helps you improve playing efficiency, accuracy, and speed.
(See Plectrum in Guitar Accessories Terms.)

Alternate Tuning

Tuning your guitar to any tuning that isn't **standard tuning** (E A D G B E), such as **drop D tuning**. Alternative guitar tunings open you up to new creative possibilities and sounds.
(See Standard Tuning and Drop D Tuning.)

Category Brackets:
These tell you the area of guitar playing or music the following term typically belongs to

See Italics:
These will guide you to related definitions in the book for deeper understanding

Fig. 1.0. Book layout

Music Genres

In this book you'll learn a brief history of the most popular music genres that feature guitars as one of the main instruments. See which ones jump out most. Exploring new styles of music can inspire you to break free from routine and become a more skilled, creative and confident guitar player.

 Remember there are other music subgenres that use the guitar, but this book focuses on the main ones you ought to know.

Chord & Scale Definitions

This book is a great place to learn the definitions of the basic chords, scales and intervals that beginner and intermediate guitar players need to know. However, if you want to take your guitar playing to the next level, check out my book *Easy Peasy Guitar Music Theory: for Beginners*. It goes in depth on music theory essentials and how to apply them to improve your playing skills.

Find it here: *www.YourGuitarBrain.com/Shop*

Helpful Icons

Do you know we remember visual cues better than just words alone? Absolutely – several studies have shown that visual aids help you better memorise and recall new information. Because of this, I've included some useful icons in this book to help you boost your learning power and remember the guitar terms more easily:

 Keep an eye out for this **Good to know** icon because it means you'll learn some handy nuggets of information.

 When there are musical examples to drive home the meaning of a term, this icon will highlight them for you.

 When you see this icon, prepare for some real-life examples that will make the definition crystal clear.

Are you ready to take a stroll down guitar vocabulary lane and learn some impressive new lingo?

Then let's rock 'n' roll amigo.

PART ONE

PARTS of a
GUITAR

Parts of an Acoustic Guitar

In this section, you'll learn the essential parts of an acoustic guitar. You'll quickly learn the names and functions of each component, so you'll be able to identify each part of your guitar and know its purpose.

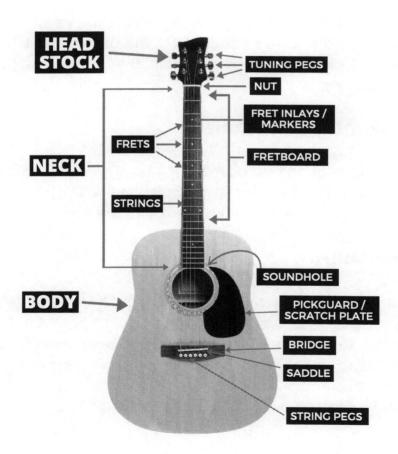

HEAD STOCK

TUNING PEGS

NUT

FRET INLAYS / MARKERS

FRETS

FRETBOARD

NECK

STRINGS

SOUNDHOLE

BODY

PICKGUARD / SCRATCH PLATE

BRIDGE

SADDLE

STRING PEGS

Body

The largest part of the instrument that includes the top (aka sound board), back, sides, and **sound hole**. The body shape and size can vary depending on the guitar's style and tonal qualities. The wood used in the body affects the acoustic guitar's **tone** and **resonance**.
(See Sound Hole, Tone [Sound] and Resonance in Glossary of Guitar Terms.)

Bridge

The piece that anchors the strings to the body and transmits the strings' vibrations to the sound board, which is the large wooden panel on the front face of the acoustic guitar.

Fret Inlays / Markers

Small dots on the fretboard that help players navigate the instrument and keep track of their hand positions. Fret inlays also add a decorative feature to a guitar.

Fretboard

Also known as the 'fingerboard', the fretboard is attached to the guitar neck and it's where you press down on the strings to produce different notes. The wood used for the fretboard can affect the **resonance** and **sustain** of the notes produced.
(See Resonance and Sustain in Glossary of Guitar Terms.)

Frets

The thin metal strips embedded in the fretboard that serve two main functions. First, they divide the neck into **intervals** that allow the guitarist to find and play particular notes. Second, they raise the string off the fretboard, allowing the player to change its length and, therefore, the note's **pitch**.
(See Interval and Pitch in Glossary of Guitar Terms.)

Headstock

The top section of the guitar neck where the tuning pegs (aka machine heads) and strings are attached. It helps to hold the strings in place and allows you to tune each string to the desired **pitch**.
(See Pitch in Glossary of Guitar Terms.)

Neck

The long, slender part of the guitar that houses the **fretboard** and supports the strings.
(See Fretboard.)

Nut

The small piece of plastic, bone, or other material at the top of the **fretboard** that the strings rest on.
(See Fretboard.)

Pickguard (aka Scratch Plate)

A protective plate on the guitar's body, underneath the sound hole, that helps to prevent scratches and dings from a plectrum (aka guitar pick) or fingers.
(See Plectrum in Guitar Accessories Terms.)

Saddle

The small piece of plastic, bone, or other material that sits in the **bridge** and provides a contact point for the guitar strings.
(See Bridge.)

Sound Hole

The circular hole on the guitar body that lets the sound of the vibrating strings resonate inside the hollow chamber and project outwards. The sound hole plays a role in determining the **tone** and volume of the guitar.
(See Tone [Sound] in Glossary of Guitar Terms.)

String Pegs

The small cylindrical pieces on the **bridge** of an acoustic guitar that help to keep the strings anchored in place.
(See Bridge.)

Strings

Metal or nylon wires that run along the length of the guitar neck and produce sound via vibration when strummed or plucked. Acoustic guitar strings are usually thicker than electric guitar strings, and the different material types include bronze, phosphor bronze, silk and steel.

Tuning Pegs (aka Machine Heads)

The geared pegs at the headstock used to adjust the tension of the strings, which in turn changes the **pitch** of the notes produced by the guitar. By turning the tuning pegs, you can either loosen or tighten individual strings to achieve the desired pitch.
(See Pitch in Glossary of Guitar Terms.)

Parts of an Electric Guitar

Get ready to become a pro at electric guitar anatomy! In this section, you'll discover the names and functions of each component and how they work together to create sound. Knowing the names of the electric guitar parts will allow you to communicate more clearly with other guitarists or repair technicians down the line.

Body

The central part of the guitar where the **pickups**, **bridge**, and other hardware are attached.
(See Pickups and Bridge.)

Bridge

The part of the guitar where the strings are anchored. It includes adjustable **saddles** that can be moved to adjust the **intonation** and string height, allowing for more precise tuning and playing.
(See Saddle and Intonation in Glossary of Guitar Terms.)

Fret Inlays / Markers

A decorative material on the side or top of a guitar's fretboard, which indicates the position of specific frets. These markers are typically made from materials such as mother of pearl, acrylic or plastic. They're placed at regular intervals along the neck, usually at the 3rd, 5th, 7th, 9th, 12th, 15th, 17th, 19th, and 21st frets.

Fretboard

The flat piece of wood attached to the neck of the guitar containing metal **frets** which help create different notes when pressed down by the fingers.
(See Frets.)

Frets

The thin metal strips embedded in the guitar fretboard which determine the **pitch** of the notes played.
(See Pitch in Glossary of Guitar Terms.)

Headstock

The top section of the guitar that houses the **tuning pegs**, which allow you to adjust the tension of the strings and, therefore, their **pitch**.
(See Tuning Pegs and Pitch in Glossary of Guitar Terms.)

Jack Input

The socket on the guitar where the cable is plugged in to connect it to an amplifier or other sound system.

Neck

The long, slender part of the guitar that connects the **headstock** to the body of the guitar. The neck houses the fretboard and supports the strings.
(See Headstock.)

Nut

A small strip of material located at the end of the fretboard near the headstock. It has slots for each string to sit in, which spaces them out to the correct distance from each other. The nut helps keep the strings in place and provides a reference point for tuning.

Pickguard (aka Scratch Plate)

A protective layer placed on the front of an electric guitar to shield its body from scratches that can occur while playing. It can also serve as a decorative element.

Pickup Selector

A switch that enables you to toggle between the different **pickups** on the guitar.
(See Pickups and Front Pickup, Back Pickup and Middle Pickup in Additional Guitar Parts Terms.)

Pickups

Devices on electric and **electro-acoustic** guitars that capture the string vibrations and convert them into an electrical signal. The main three types of pickups are **single-coil**, **humbucker**, and **P90 pickups**. Each one has a unique sound and **tone**.
(See Single-Coil, Humbucker and P90 Pickups in Additional Guitar Parts Terms and Electro-Acoustic Guitar and Tone [Sound] in Glossary of Guitar Terms.)

Saddle

A small component on the **bridge** of an electric guitar that helps to support and position the strings, ensuring that they stay in tune and that the **intonation** is correct.
(See Bridge and Intonation in Glossary of Guitar Terms.)

Strap Button

Small pegs or screws on the body of the guitar that provide attachment points for a guitar strap.

Strings

Metal wires stretched across a guitar's **neck** and **body**. When plucked or strummed, they vibrate and create sound waves amplified through the guitar's **pickups** and amplifier. An electric guitar usually has six strings, although some models have seven or eight.
(See Neck, Body and Pickups.)

Tuning Pegs

Also called 'machine heads', these are small geared devices located on the guitar's **headstock** that adjust the strings' tension and tuning.
(See Headstock.)

Volume and Tone Controls

Knobs and switches on a guitar that serve the same function as knobs on a stereo system; they allow you to adjust the sound of your guitar to your liking. The volume control adjusts the overall loudness, while the tone control lets you shape the **EQ** (equalisation) by boosting or cutting specific **frequencies**.
(See EQ and Frequency in Glossary of Guitar Terms.)

Additional Guitar Parts Terms

Back Pickup

Also known as the 'bridge' or 'treble' pickup (an electric sound converter) this pickup is located near the **bridge** of the guitar and produces a bright and cutting sound ideal for playing **melodies** and **guitar solos**.
(See Bridge in Parts of an Electric Guitar and Melody and Guitar, Solo in Glossary of Guitar Terms.)

Bigsby Vibrato (aka Bigsby Tremolo)

The Bigsby Vibrato is a metal arm attached to an electric guitar that allows the player to gently bend or wiggle the guitar's strings, slightly altering their **pitch**. It's often used in **rockabilly** and **country music** and is found on guitar brands like Gretsch, Eastwood, and Gibson.
(See Tremolo Arm and Pitch, Rockabilly and Country Music in Glossary of Guitar Terms.)

Binding

Strips of decorative material, often made of wood or plastic, that run along the edges of a guitar **body** and **neck**.
(See Body and Neck in Parts of an Acoustic Guitar.)

Cutaway

A section of the guitar **body** near the **neck** that has been 'cut away' to allow easier access to the higher **frets** on the **fretboard**. There are several types of guitar cutaways; the main ones include single, double, Venetian and Florentine cutaways.
(See Body, Neck, Frets and Fretboard in Parts of an Acoustic Guitar.)

Floyd Rose "Whammy Bar"

A type of **tremolo arm** used on electric guitars. It was developed by Floyd Rose and allows the guitarist to change the **pitch** of the strings by moving the **bridge** up or down, producing a unique "whammy" or **vibrato** sound effect. They're a popular choice for guitarists who perform **lead guitar** techniques such as **dive bombs** and vibrato.
(See Tremolo Arm and Bridge in Parts of an Electric Guitar, Pitch, Lead Guitar, Dive Bomb and Vibrato in Glossary of Guitar Terms.)

Front Pickup

Also known as the 'neck' or 'rhythm' pickup, this pickup (an electric sound converter) is located near the **neck** of the guitar. It is known for producing a warm and full-bodied **tone,** making it a favourite among blues and jazz guitarists.
(See Neck in Parts of an Electric Guitar and Tone [Sound] in Glossary of Guitar Terms.)

Humbucker Pickup

A type of pickup (an electric sound converter) with two magnetic coils that cancel out the hum and noise of a guitar signal. Known for its warm and thick sound, the Gibson Les Paul is a famous guitar with two humbucker pickups. Examples of iconic humbucker-loving guitarists include Black Sabbath's Tony Iommi and Slash from the band Guns 'n' Roses.

Middle Pickup

This pickup (an electric sound converter) is located in the middle of the guitar. It can be used independently or combined with the **front** or **back pickups** to create a range of sounds; from fat and punchy to **clean** and **jangly**, respectively.
(See Front and Back Pickup and Clean and Jangly in Slang for Guitar Sounds.)

P90 Pickup

This versatile pickup (an electric sound converter) is used for various music styles, from **rock** to **country**. Known for its fat and gritty sound, it has a larger coil than **single-coil pickups**, producing a thicker sound with more **mid-range** and bass. Renowned guitarists that have used P90s include Carlos Santana and rock 'n' roller Chuck Berry.
(See Single-Coil Pickup and Rock and Country Music in Glossary of Guitar Terms and Mid-Range in Slang for Guitar Sounds.)

Single-Coil Pickup

A type of pickup (an electric sound converter) known for its bright and clear sound. It has a single magnetic coil that picks up the strings' vibrations and sends them to an amplifier. Single-coil pickups are associated with makes like Fender Stratocaster guitars, popularised by guitar legends such as Jimi Hendrix and John Mayer.

Tremolo Arm

A device attached to an electric guitar that creates a **vibrato** or **pitch**-bending effect. The tremolo arm was named by Leo Fender, founder of Fender Guitars. Playing a note and pressing down on the tremolo arm lowers the note's pitch, and releasing it returns it to its original pitch. You create vibrato by playing a note and moving the tremolo arm back and forth.
(See Vibrato and Pitch in Glossary of Guitar Terms.)

 Good to know: The name "tremolo arm" was incorrectly appointed by Fender. "Tremolo" means a modulation in *volume*, not pitch. Oops!

Truss Rod

A metal bar that runs the length of a guitar **neck** from the **nut** to where the neck joins the **body**. The job of the truss rod is to help balance the effect of string tension on the neck via adjustments to the guitar's **neck relief.**
(See Neck, Nut and Body in Parts of an Electric Guitar and Neck Relief in Glossary of Guitar Terms.)

PART TWO

GLOSSARY of GUITAR TERMS

Glossary of Guitar Terms

Whether you're a beginner or have some experience playing guitar, this section is jam-packed with definitions of frequently used guitar terms that will simplify your learning journey. Let's jump in and expand our guitar lingo!

12-Bar Blues [Songwriting & Composition]

A popular chord progression used in genres such as **blues**, **rock 'n' roll**, and **jazz**. It has 12 **bars** (aka measures) that follow a key's I-IV-V pattern of chords. Despite the name, the number of bars can vary in music labelled as "12-bar blues". What does remain the same is the distinctive 'bluesy' **rhythm** and **groove**.
(See Bar, Key Signature, Rhythm, Blues, Rock and Roll and Jazz Music and Groove in General Slang Terms.)

3/4 Size Guitar [Guitar Types]

A small guitar with an overall length of under 36 inches and an average scale length between 20 to 24 inches. The dimensions depend on the guitar maker, as no fixed-size standards exist. The term "3/4" doesn't actually refer to the size of the guitar; it's an old naming convention for stringed instruments that has stuck.

Accents (aka Stresses) [Playing Technique]

A note or beat of music with a **dynamic** push that creates a sense of rhythm or emphasis.
(See Dynamics.)

Acoustic Guitar [Guitar Types]

A guitar made from wood with a hollow body that produces sound from the vibration of six strings acoustically. The wood used to make an acoustic guitar largely influences its sound and price.

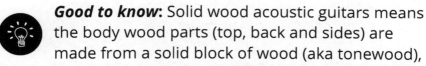 ***Good to know***: Solid wood acoustic guitars means the body wood parts (top, back and sides) are made from a solid block of wood (aka tonewood), which is often rare and not eco-friendly. Examples include ebony, mahogany and rosewood.
The great news is you can choose many stunning-sounding alternative *and* sustainable tonewoods for your next guitar.
*(See Tonewood and **Alternative & Sustainable Guitar Woods** near the end of the book.)*

Laminate acoustic guitars are cheaper and more sustainable than solid wood guitars because they're made from shaved and layered wood, which is made to look like a solid piece of wood.

Action (aka String Action)

The distance between the strings and the fretboard on guitars and other stringed instruments. The action plays a big role in how easy it feels to play a guitar and how clear it sounds. Too low an action will cause string buzz, and too high makes the guitar more challenging to play.

Take your guitar to a good **luthier** if you don't want to tackle alterations yourself and risk botching it up.
(See Neck Relief and Luthier and Truss Rod in Additional Guitar Parts Terms.)

Good to know: Action often changes over time due to factors such as humidity or extreme temperature fluctuations, which cause the guitar wood to expand and contract. Adjustments are easily made via tweaks to the **truss rod** and **neck relief**. Using a de-humidifier will also prevent such damage.
(See De-Humidifier in Guitar Accessories Terms.)

Alternate Picking [Playing Technique]

The name of a technique where you pluck the guitar strings with a **plectrum** (aka guitar pick) using alternating downstrokes and upstrokes. This picking technique helps you improve playing efficiency, accuracy, and speed.
(See Plectrum in Guitar Accessories Terms.)

Alternate Tuning

Tuning your guitar to any tuning that isn't **standard tuning** (E A D G B E), such as **drop D tuning**. Alternative guitar tunings open you up to new creative possibilities and sounds on the guitar.
(See Standard Tuning and Drop D Tuning.)

Archtop Guitar [Guitar Types]

A favourite with jazz and blues guitarists, an archtop is a type of **hollow** or **semi-hollow** body guitar. Usually electric with distinctive f-hole designs carved into the body, archtops made their way into the live music scene as early as the 1920s.
(See Hollow-Body and Semi-Hollow Guitar.)

Arpeggio [Playing Technique]

A technique where a chord is played one note at a time rather than being strummed or plucked simultaneously. Arpeggios typically involve playing each chord note in sequence, usually in an ascending and descending pattern.
They can help to elevate even the simplest **chord progression**, add variation to **melodies** and **solos**, and sharpen your picking accuracy tenfold.
(See Chord Progression, Melody and Solo, Guitar.)

Arrangement [Songwriting & Composition]

The structure and composition of a piece of music. In **classical music**, an arrangement means an adaption of an existing composition into a new creative expression. For example, when a **classical guitarist** plays the vocal melody of a song as an instrumental.
(See Classical Music and Classical Guitar Music.)

Articulation [Playing Technique]

The way a note, chord or phrase is to be played using performance parameters, such as **accents**, **dynamics**, **attack** and **slurs**.
(See Accents, Dynamics, Attack and Slur.)

Attack [Playing Technique]

Describes how hard or soft a musician plays their instrument. In a more general sense, "attack" can refer to the overall energy and intention behind a musician's playing. A player with a strong attack might be described as passionate and **dynamic**.
(See Dynamics.)

Auditorium Guitar [Guitar Types]

A type of acoustic guitar shape that is a cross between a **dreadnaught** and **concert** acoustic guitar. The auditorium has a slim body depth and curved waist (similar to a **parlour** guitar). As its name suggests, a grand auditorium shaped guitar is a larger version of its auditorium sister. It suits most guitarists playing styles, from pop song strummer to folksy fingerpicker.
(See Dreadnaught, Concert and Parlour Guitar.)

Augmented Chord [Music Theory]

A chord with an unsettling and uneasy sound. Think of it as a **major chord** with a raised 5th **interval**, which makes its **interval formula** 1-3-#5. To give you an example, the notes in a C augmented chord (aka Caug, C+) are C-E-G#.

Augmented chords are a type of **triad**. *(See Major Chord, Interval, Interval Formula and Triad.)*

Bar (aka Measure) [Rhythm]

A unit of musical time that organises the **rhythm** and **melody** of a song. Each bar contains a specific number of **beats**, which are typically grouped together to form a repeating pattern throughout the song. For example, a piece of music in **4/4 time** has four beats per bar, while a piece in **3/4 time** has three beats per bar.
(See Rhythm, Melody, Beat and Time Signature.)

Barre Chord

A chord shape played on a guitar (and other stringed instruments) by using one or more fingers to press down on multiple strings across a single fret. Barre chords are typically **movable chord** shapes we can shift and play on various positions of the fretboard. The word "barre" comes from the French word "barré", which means "barred".
(See Movable Chord.)

Beat [Rhythm]

The building blocks of **rhythm** in music, which are the regular, recurring pulses you can feel or hear. We group beats into **bars** (aka measures) and they provide a sense of timing, helping listeners stay on track with the song.
(See Rhythm and Bar.)

Bebop Music (aka Bebop Blues) [Genre]

A style of fast-paced **jazz-blues music** developed in the early 1940s that features flashy **improvisation**, complex chord progressions and virtuoso playing. The emergence of bebop, led by pioneers such as Charlie Parker and Dizzy Gillespie, was a reaction against the conventional jazz of the **swing** era. These musicians aimed to elevate jazz into an art form and explore new musical frontiers. *(See Improvisation and Jazz, Blues and Swing Music.)*

 Bebop Music Examples: *Guitarists:* Charlie Christian, Jimmy Raney, Wes Montgomery, Tal Farlow.

Bend [Playing Technique]

A technique used in **lead guitar** playing that involves picking a note and bending the string up or down with one or more fingers. Most guitar bends change the **pitch** of a note by one **semitone** (half step), one **tone** (whole step) or somewhere in between. It depends on the vibe the guitarist is going for. Adding a bend to a **melody line** can inject a sense of expressiveness and vibrancy when performed with good **feel**. *(See Lead Guitar, Pitch, Semitone, Tone, Melody and Feel.)*

Blue Note [Music Theory]

A note **interval** added to a **pentatonic scale** that gives **blues music** its characteristic flavour. In the minor pentatonic scale, the blue note is typically the **flat fifth**

(♭5) or **major third** (M3). In the case of the major pentatonic scale, the blue note is the **flat third** (♭3).
(See Interval, Pentatonic Scale, Blues Music, Flat Fifth, Major Third and Flat Third.)

Bluegrass Music [Genre]

With roots in **country** and **folk music**, bluegrass developed in the mid-1940s and features fast-paced instrumentals played on acoustic stringed instruments. Solo virtuosity is a key element of the genre, with banjo, mandolin, guitar, and fiddle taking centre stage.

Legendary musician Earl Scruggs introduced the world to a fast fingerstyle banjo technique synonymous with the bluegrass sound dubbed the 'Scruggs Style'. Also known as the '3-finger banjo style', the technique uses guitar picks on the thumb, middle, and index fingers.

Earl didn't invent the playing technique, but he made it his own by refining and redefining an existing style. The bluegrass genre was named after "Bill Monroe and his Bluegrass Boys", of which Scruggs was a member.
(See Country and Folk Music.)

 Bluegrass Music Examples: *Artists:* Bill Monroe, Earl Scruggs, Lester Flatt, Chubby Wise, Howard Watts.

Blues Music [Genre]

This musical genre has roots in the expressive music crafted by enslaved Africans who were forcibly transported to the American Deep South during the 1800s, following the end of the Civil War. Like many other pioneering musical genres of the 19th and 20th centuries, the history of blues music is deeply entwined with racial, social and political turmoil.

The subjugated African people forced to work on Southern plantations sang songs known as 'field hollers' and 'work songs'. These songs were characterised by emotive lyrics, mournful melodies, and a **call-and-response** style. They inspired the modern blues that we know today. While the lyrics of blues music often touch on themes of hardship and sorrow, this genre is also about celebrating raw emotion and championing the message of triumphing over adversity.

Blues music is the result of a fusion of various musical styles, including African spirituals, chants, ragtime, and African drum music. Along with the creation of the **blues scale**, other distinct features of this genre include the **12-bar blues** chord progression, swinging **rhythms**, and heartfelt **guitar solos**.

Since its inception in the Mississippi Delta, blues music has captivated generations of guitarists worldwide and has given rise to a multitude of *sub-genres that that will likely continue to thrive long after we're gone.
(See Call and Response, Blues Scale, 12-Bar Blues, Rhythm and Solo, Guitar.)

Blues Music Examples: *Guitarists:* Blind Lemon Jefferson, Robert Johnson, Odetta, Buddy Guy, B.B. King, Muddy Waters, Freddie King, Beverly "Guitar" Watkins, Jimmy Reed.

Good to know: * Prominent subgenres of blues music include boogie-woogie, jump blues, country blues, blues rock, Chicago blues, Delta blues, New Orleans blues, Texas blues, and many more. Wow, now that's a whole lotta blues!

Blues Scale [Music Theory]

A scale used in **blues music** that typically includes six notes, with the addition of the **blue note**, which is a lowered fifth **interval** (♭5). The **flat fifth** gives the scale a distinctive sound that is often associated with the genre. The blues scale is also commonly used in **rock**, **jazz**, and other forms of music.
(See Blue Note, Interval, Flat Fifth, Blues, Rock and Jazz Music.)

BPM

An abbreviation for beats per minute, which is a unit of measurement used to describe the tempo of music. For instance, if a song is played at 115 bpm, there are 115 beats in one minute.

Bridge [Songwriting & Composition]

A bridge is a section of a song that connects two parts of an arrangement, such as a **verse** and **chorus**. In the latter position, a bridge is also known as a 'pre-chorus'. When it

occurs in the middle of a song, a bridge is called a 'middle eight' in certain parts of the world, such as the United Kingdom.
(See Verse and Chorus.)

Call and Response

A musical phrase that is either sung or played by two different people (or a group of people). This form of musical punctuation is found across many genres of music and has its roots in various musical traditions, such as African spiritual songs, **folk** and **gospel music**.
(See Folk and Gospel Music.)

 Examples of call and response:

1.   **Church music – *Call*:** The pastor sings to the church congregation, "Can I get an Amen?"
Response: The crowd sings back, "Amen."
2.   **Pop music –** the chorus of *Wanna be Starting Something* by Michael Jackson:
Call: Michael sings, "It's too high to get over."
Response: Backing vocals sing, "(Yeah yeah.)"

Chord [Music Theory]

A group of notes taken from a scale (usually three or more) played together that produces a particular sound and mood. Common chord types include **major, minor, diminished**, major 7th, sus4, dominant 7th, and so on.
(See Major, Minor and Diminished Chord.)

Chord Chart (aka Chord Diagram)

A visual aid typically seen in chord song sheets that shows the shape of a chord, including the frets and which fingers you use to play the chord.

Chord Inversion [Music Theory]

A chord shape whose note order has been shuffled around, so the **root note** is no longer the lowest (bass) note in the chord. Take your guitar playing up a notch with chord inversions for a fresh and exciting twist on traditional chord shapes.
(See Root Note.)

Chord Progression

A series of chords, such as C-G-Am-F, that typically repeats and forms a specific section of a song (e.g. the verse, bridge, or chorus.) Chord progressions add structure to music, serving as the **harmonic** foundation for a song's **melody** and lyrics.
(See Harmony and Melody.)

Chord Voicing [Music Theory]

Refers to the order of the individual notes within a chord. E.g. CMajor7 chord notes = C-E-G-B, could be rearranged and played as C-E-B-G. These are different voicings of the same chord.

Chorus [Songwriting & Composition]

The main section of a song often characterised by a catchy sing-along **melody** that builds in intensity and features a fuller **arrangement** than previous parts. A chorus is typically enhanced by more instruments.
(See Melody and Arrangement.)

Chromatic [Music Theory]

A type of musical scale that contains 12 notes arranged one **semitone** (aka half step) away from each other. For example, the C chromatic scale notes are C, C#, D, D#, E, F, F#, G, G#, A, A# and B.
(See Semitone.)

Circle of Fifths [Music Theory]

A reference chart that shows how the 12 different musical **key signatures**, **scales** and **chords** fit together. It's a handy tool for anyone who's not comfortable with reading **music notation**.
(See Key Signature, Scale, Chord and Music Notation.)

Classical Guitar (aka Nylon-String or Spanish)
[Guitar Types]

A type of acoustic guitar that features a broad neck and is commonly used for playing **fingerstyle classical guitar music** and Spanish music. It should be noted that there is no difference between the terms "Spanish" and "classical" guitar, and they're often used interchangeably.
Classical guitars have nylon strings (traditionally made from animal gut) that produce a mellow and soft tone.

The G, B and high E strings are nylon, while the low E, A, and D strings have nylon cores with a metal coating.
(See Fingerstyle and Classical Guitar Music.)

Classical Guitar Music [Genre]

This genre is characterised largely by performances of classical pieces spanning from the Renaissance era (approximately 1400 to 1600) to the modern day (1920-present). Nowadays, classical guitarists have broadened their repertoire to include classical music from various parts of the world, including Spain, South America, India, Asia, and beyond.

The mixture of diverse cultural styles and popular music genres, such as **jazz** and **rhythm and blues**, is a hallmark of contemporary classical guitarists. For instance, Cuban-born classical guitar maestro Leo Brouwer was captivated by powerful African Yoruba ritual music, and so blended Afro-Cuban and classical European elements to create a unique fusion style.

With the ongoing trend of mixing old styles with new ones and the exceptional level of musicianship, the world of classical guitar music is constantly evolving in an exciting direction.
(See Jazz and Rhythm and Blues Music.)

 Classical Music Examples: *Early Era Guitarists:* Matteo Carcassi, Francisco Tárrega, Justin Holland, Mauro Giuliani | *Modern Era Guitarists:* Ana Vidović, Sean Shibe, Xuefei Yang, Sungha Jung.

Classical Music [Genre]

The broadest genre of music that dates back hundreds of years and has a foothold in the history of many global civilisations. The term "classical music" generally refers to the music of the Western world in a specific period (mid-1700s to 1820). In reality, the term is commonly used to describe a traditional style of music composed in any country.

Classical music is an enduring genre that has fascinated listeners for centuries, whether it's a Roman lyre sonata composed in 100 BC or Handel's bombastic oratorio *Messiah* from 1741. As a result, Western classical music is closely associated with various historical periods, which are listed below.

Classical Music Eras: Medieval, Renaissance, Baroque, Classical, Romantic, 20th Century and Modern.

Classical music encompasses an array of **music scores**. These scores are performed by orchestras for operas, chamber and choral ensembles, quartets and quintets, and also feature in solo performances, such as piano and classical guitar concertos.
(See Classical Guitar Music and Music Score.)

 Classical Music Examples: *Composers*: Frédéric Chopin, Edward Elgar, Ethel Smyth, Ludovico Einaudi.

Common Time [Rhythm]

Another term used to describe **4/4 time signature**, which tells us there are four **quarter note** beats (aka crotchets) in every bar. The symbol for common time used in music notation looks like this:
(See Time Signature and Quarter Note.)

Concert Guitar [Guitar Types]

This style of guitar strikes a balance between the smaller **parlour guitars** and larger **dreadnought-style** acoustics. It has a bigger body that results in a fuller sound than the former but less richness than the latter. It is the baby brother to the **grand concert guitar**.
(See Parlour, Dreadnought and Grand Concert Guitar.)

Consonance [Music Theory]

Chords, **melodies** or **scales** that contain note **intervals** which sound good together and create a feeling of stability and ease for the listener. An example of a chord with a consonant vibe is the jolly and happy-sounding **major chord**.
(See Melody, Scale, Interval and Major Chord.)

Country Music [Genre]

A genre abundant with outstanding guitarists; country music (formerly called 'country and western music') originated in the rural areas of the southern United States in the early-20th century.

Despite being considered the original homegrown American genre, the origins of country music are a culturally diverse melting pot of many styles. They include Celtic folk (aka Appalachian folk), **jazz**, **blues** and West African **folk music**.

Country music has given us some of American music history's most influential and successful artists, such as Johnny Cash, Willie Nelson and Garth Brooks. Not just one-trick ponies, many country musicians have also crossed over to different genres and gained widespread recognition. Dolly Parton and Taylor Swift are shining examples of successful crossover artists, demonstrating not just their impressive singing abilities but also their often overlooked guitar playing skills. Ladies, we salute your versatile talent.

(See Jazz, Blues and Folk Music.)

Good to know: Country music's iconic banjo has its origins in traditional instruments that were brought to the Americas and the Caribbean by enslaved Africans.

Country Music Examples: *Guitarists:* Chet Atkins, Vince Gill, Brad Paisley, Merle Travis, Norman Blake.

Cut Time [Rhythm]

A musical meter with two half notes per bar that lasts the same duration as four **quarter notes**. Also known as 'alla

breve', the symbol for cut time, that represents the **time signature** 2/2, looks like this:
(See Quarter Note and Time Signature).

DADGAD Tuning

An alternative way to tune the guitar where the open strings are tuned to the notes D, A, D, G, A, and D – instead of **standard tuning**. A famous song that uses this tuning is *Kashmir* by the rock band Led Zeppelin.
(See Standard Tuning.)

Degree, Scale [Music Theory]

A degree in music is a number that tells you how far a note is from the start of a scale. For example, in the C **major scale**, C is the first degree, D is the second degree, E is the third degree, and so on. Degrees can help you create catchy **melodies** and chords because they show you which notes sound good together in a specific scale and key.
(See Major Scale and Melody.)

Deluxe Guitar [Guitar Types]

A higher-end or upgraded version of a **standard acoustic guitar** with additional features or a more refined design. To name a few examples of such elaborate features, a deluxe acoustic guitar may have more decorative inlays, a premium wood construction, or advanced electronic **pickups**.
(See Standard Guitar and Pickups in Parts of An Electric Guitar.)

Diatonic [Music Theory]

This word comes from ancient Greek music theory and means *"through (whole) tones"*. Today, the term is most often used to describe **melodies** and **harmonies** that use notes solely from a specific **key signature**.
(See Tone, Melody, Harmony and Key Signature.)

Diatonic Chords [Music Theory]

Chords constructed from notes belonging to a specific scale **key**, such as the **major** and **natural minor scales**.
(See Key Signature, Major and Minor Scale.)

Diatonic Scale [Music Theory]

A scale constructed from five **tones** and two **semitone** intervals, such as the **majo**r and natural **minor scales**.
(See Tone, Semitone, Major and Minor Scale.)

Diminished Chord [Music Theory]

A chord with a tense and edgy sound. Think of it as a **minor chord** with a **flattened 5th** interval, making its **interval formula** 1-♭3-♭5. For example, the notes in a C diminished chord (aka Cdim, C°) are C-E♭-G♭. Diminished chords are also known as '**triads**'.
(See Minor Chord, Flat Fifth, Interval Formula and Triad.)

Dissonance [Music Theory]

Chords, melodies or scales that contain note **intervals** that sound like they clash, which creates a tense and

unstable feeling in the listener. An example of a chord with a dissonant vibe is the eerie-sounding **augmented chord**, which has no **perfect fifth interval**.
(See Interval, Augmented Chord and Perfect Fifth.)

Dive Bomb [Playing Technique]

A technique where the guitarist uses the **tremolo arm** (aka **whammy bar**) to create a sudden drop in note **pitch**. This method gives the guitar a dramatic and expressive sound heard mainly in **metal** and **rock**.
(See Pitch, Metal and Rock Music and Tremolo Arm and Floyd Rose "Whammy Bar" in Additional Guitar Parts Terms.)

Double Stop [Playing Technique]

Playing two notes at the same time. Also called a 'dyad', double stops are used in **rhythm** and **lead guitar** playing. They're a handy way of transitioning between chords and notes. Listen to the recognisable intro **riff** on Van Morrison's *Brown Eyed Girl* for an example of double stops in action.
(See Rhythm and Lead Guitar and Riff in General Slang Terms.)

Downbeat [Rhythm]

The first **beat** in a **bar** (aka measure), which is accented stronger than the other beats. The definition of a downbeat is somewhat flexible; many musicians refer to all beats in a bar occurring on the count as downbeats. Bolded downbeats can be seen here:
1 and **2** and **3** and **4** and.
(See Beat and Bar.)

Dreadnought Guitar [Guitar Types]

The most commonly used acoustic guitar body shape, originally designed in 1916 by guitar manufacturer C.F. Martin & Company (you'll probably know them as 'Martin'). With its large body size, a dreadnought produces a full tone with good **low-end** and balanced **mid** and **top end**, perfect for strumming and picking. *(See Low-End, Mid-Range and High-End in Slang for Guitar Sounds.)*

Drop D Tuning

An alternative way to tune the guitar which is popular in genres such as **rock**, **metal** and **grunge**. The low E string is tuned one **tone** (whole step) down in **pitch** to a D note, instead of the standard E note. *(See Tone, Pitch and Rock, Metal and Grunge Music.)*

Dynamics [Playing Technique]

In guitar playing this describes the range of volume and intensity of sound that a guitarist can achieve through their playing This includes variations in volume, **accents**, and **articulation**. *(See Accents and Articulation.)*

Ear Training

The process of training your ears to recognise and reproduce musical elements, such as **melodies**, **harmonies**, and **rhythms**, without using **sheet music** or guitar-specific notation called **tablature**. Ear training is

essential for guitar players who don't read music, and you develop the skill by repeating listening exercises.
(See Melody, Harmony, Rhythm, Sheet Music and Tablature.)

Economy of Movement [Playing Technique]

A phrase that describes using efficient **good playing technique** (i.e. minimal motion on both hands) to banish sloppy, messy playing. Two examples of economy of movement include keeping the **fretting** hand fingers close to the fretboard and using the ideal amount of motion in the strumming arm and wrist.
(See Fretting and Good Technique.)

Economy Picking [Playing Technique]

A picking technique that combines **alternate picking** with a bit of **sweep picking** to help improve picking efficiency and flow. For example, instead of picking in a *down/up/down/up* motion between each note, you would play some notes with consecutive picks in the same direction: *down/up down/up/down/down/up.*
(See Alternate Picking and Sweep Picking.)

Eighth Note (aka Quaver, 1/8th) [Rhythm]

An eighth note (American) or quaver (British) is a type of **note value** where a single note lasts the duration of one-eighth of a 4-beat **bar** (half a beat). It has a time value equal to half a **quarter note**, meaning there are eight eighth beats per bar.

The musical notation symbol that represents an 1/8 note looks like this:
(See Note Value, Bar and Quarter Note.)

Electric Guitar [Guitar Types]

A guitar that uses electronics in the form of **pickups**, which transform string vibrations into electrical signals sent through an amplifier to generate sound. They commonly have six strings but can have more.
The electric guitar revolutionised the music industry with its ability to produce louder and more versatile sounds than traditional **acoustic guitars**. They played a significant role in shaping the sound of many music genres, from **blues**, **rock**, and **jazz** to **metal** and beyond.
(See Acoustic Guitar, Blues, Rock, Jazz and Metal Music and Pickups in Parts of an Electric Guitar.)

Electro-Acoustic Guitar [Guitar Types]

An acoustic guitar that has been outfitted with electronic **pickups**, which allows you to play it amplified or unplugged for that classic acoustic vibe.
(See Pickups in Parts of an Electric Guitar.)

Enharmonic Notes [Music Theory]

Notes that have the same **pitch** but have different note names. Example: G#/A♭.
(See Pitch.)

EQ (aka Equalisation)

Adjusting the balance of various **frequency** ranges in an audio signal. EQ frequencies range from low sub-bass (anything under 60Hz) to **high-end** air frequencies (14kHz and above).
(See Frequency and High-End in Slang for Guitar Sounds.)

Extended Chord [Music Theory]

Chords that add spice and colour beyond the basic **triad** chords. Used in styles such as **jazz**, **funk** and **classical music**, extended chords (aka chord extensions) contain extra notes above the seventh **degree** of the scale they're made from.
They have one of these numbers at the end of their name: 9, 11 and 13. For example, Cmaj9, Fm11, E7(♯9).
(See Triad, Degree, Scale and Jazz, Funk, and Classical Music.)

Feedback

The piercing, often undesirable noise that occurs when the amplified sound from a guitar's **pickups** is fed back into an amplifier, creating a sound loop. It's a recognised term in guitar playing and audio engineering.
Some guitarists intentionally use feedback to create wild dramatic effects, while others prefer to tame it for a more polite, clean sound.
(See Pickups in Parts of an Electric Guitar.)

Feel [Rhythm] [Playing Technique]

To play with great "feel" means conveying emotion via creativity, playing technique, sense of **rhythm** and musical expression. It goes beyond the notes you're playing or singing.
Playing the guitar "with feel" isn't a science that can be taught; it is about engaging the right brain (intuitive and visionary) rather than simply the left brain (logical and analytical).
(See Rhythm.)

 Example of feel in use:

> "I love how he plays the blues; he puts so much emotion and **feel** into it that the music touches your soul."

Finger-Per-Fret [Playing Technique]

A method of playing the guitar where each finger of the **fretting** hand is assigned to a specific fret, allowing for efficient and accurate finger placement. This skill helps you play **scales**, **melodies** and fast phrases better.
(See Fretting, Scale and Melody.)

Fingerstyle (aka Finger Picking) [Playing Technique]

Playing the guitar by plucking the strings with the fingertips and thumb or with picks attached to the fingers. You can play fingerstyle on any type of guitar, but

the style is mainly associated with **acoustic**, **classical** and **flamenco guitars**.
(See Acoustic, Classical and Flamenco Guitar.)

Flamenco Guitar [Guitar Types]

A small type of acoustic guitar similar to a **classical** and Spanish guitar but with different build features. Built lighter and thinner than classical guitars, flamenco guitars are designed to produce a more percussive sound to suit the **attack,** speed, and **rhythmic accents** traditional flamenco guitarists use. The **action** is lower than on a classical guitar to prevent string buzz.
(See Classical Guitar, Rhythm, Attack, and Action.)

Flat Fifth, Interval [Music Theory]

A flat fifth is when you lower the fifth note of a **scale** by one **semitone** (one guitar fret). For example, if the **root note** is C, the 5th note is G, and the flat fifth is G flat (G♭.) The flat fifth can add an edgy quality to **melodies** or **chords**. Symbol: ♭5
(See Scale, Semitone, Root Note, Melody and Chord.)

Flat Third, Interval [Music Theory]

A flat third is the **interval** between two notes four **semitones** apart. In the **key** of C major, for example, a flat third is between C and E♭. Flat thirds are often used to create a sense of sadness or melancholy in music. Symbol: ♭3
(See Interval, Semitone and Key Signature.)

Flat Top [Guitar Types]

A term used to describe a type of guitar body with a flat top, as opposed to an **archtop**. The average **standard acoustic guitar** falls into the flat-top category.
(See Archtop and Standard Guitar.)

Flatpicking (aka Plectrum Picking) [Playing Technique]

Picking individual notes on the strings of a guitar with a guitar pick rather than with your fingers. Flatpicking generally produces a crisp and clear sound that contrasts with the softer **tone** of **fingerstyle** guitar playing.
(See Tone [Sound] and Fingerstyle.)

Folk Music [Genre]

Traditional music from a specific region or culture that is usually passed on by people or within families. Taken from the German word "volk", which means "the people", folk music usually features stringed instruments, such as the fiddle, acoustic guitar, banjo, and zither, depending on the country of origin.

Folk often reflects a community's history, customs, and beliefs and may incorporate elements of storytelling, dance, and other rich cultural traditions.

 Folk Music Examples: *Guitarists:* Woody Guthrie, John Fahey, Joni Mitchell, Lead Belly, Bob Dylan.

Fretting [Playing Technique]

When you press down on the strings of an instrument, such as a guitar, ukulele, or mandolin, with your fingers to play notes and chord shapes. The left hand is the fretting hand for right-handed players, and the right hand is the fretting hand for lefties.

Frequency

The rate at which a sound wave vibrates as measured in Hertz (Hz). Each string on a guitar is tuned to a specific frequency. For example, the low E string (6th) is tuned to 82.4Hz, and the A string (5th) is 110Hz.

Full-Size Guitar (aka Standard Guitar) [Guitar Types]

A guitar with an average **scale length** between 24.5 and 25.5 inches and a total body length of approximately 38 inches. These measurements are used for most acoustic and electric guitars, with variations depending on the make and model of the guitar.
(See Scale Length.)

Fundamental Note / Pitch [Music Theory]

The lowest **frequency** a note produces that your ear perceives. For example, when you play the note on the 3rd fret of the A string on a guitar, the fundamental **pitch** is a C note. However, there are also additional **harmonics** and **overtones** present.
(See Frequency, Pitch, Harmonics and Overtone.)

Funk Music [Genre]

With a distinctive blend of **syncopated rhythms**, grooving bass lines, and 'funky' electric guitar **riffs**, **funk music** is a genre that seamlessly merges soul, **R&B**, and **jazz**. The term "funk" first appeared in 1900s jazz circles to describe a distinct pulsing groove.

Funk found its feet as a standalone genre in African-American communities in the 1960s, and today its influence can be heard across multiple music genres.
(See Syncopation, Funk, Rhythm and Blues and Jazz Music and Riff in General Slang Terms.)

Funk Music Examples: *Artists:* James Brown, Chaka Khan, Sly and The Family Stone, Prince | *Guitarists:* Nile Rodgers, Eddie Hazel, Jimmy Nolen, Al McKay.

Glissando [Playing Technique]

A technique that involves sliding a finger or **slide** along the guitar strings to create a smooth and continuous transition between notes.
(See Slide Guitar.)

Good Technique [Playing Technique]

Good technique is like the secret sauce of guitar playing. It's the magic that happens when you play with ease, precision, and expression, creating a seamless flow of music. It's about having control in both hands, using the most efficient fingerings and motions (aka **economy of**

movement), playing with great **feel** in sync with the tempo and the groove, and producing clear and consistent notes.

Good technique takes time and practise to achieve, but it's worth it. Nothing beats being able to play your favourite songs flawlessly.

(See Economy of Movement and Feel.)

Gospel Music (aka Church Music) [Genre]

Gospel music, a genre of Christian music, is known for its mighty layered vocal harmonies and Christian-themed lyrics that celebrate faith, salvation, and the praise of God. While often performed by choirs, it's not limited to this type of ensemble. Gospel music evolved from the spiritual songs sung by enslaved Africans in the American South, **folk music** and traditional European American hymns that trace back to the 18th Century.

The exuberant soulful style of gospel music we recognise today arose in the mid-1900s and infused elements of popular secular music, such as **jazz**, **R&B** and ragtime. Whether performed a cappella (without instruments) or with musical accompaniment, gospel music continues to have a powerful influence on various contemporary music genres.

(See Folk, Jazz and Rhythm and Blues Music.)

 Gospel Music Examples: *Composers and Artists:* Rev. Charles A. Tindley, Reverend Gary Davis, Thomas A. Dorsey, Aretha Franklin.

Grace Note [Playing Technique]

A subtle note **articulation** where you briefly play a note that acts as a musical bridge (aka **passing tone**) that connects two chords or notes in a musical **phrase**. Grace notes are normally expressive playing techniques, such as **hammer-ons** or **slides**.
(See Articulation, Passing Tone, Phrase, Hammer-On and Slide.)

Grand Auditorium (See Auditorium Guitar)

Grand Concert Guitar [Guitar Types]

A small-sized acoustic guitar with a narrow waist and short **scale length**, which is the most common type of **concert guitar**. Because of its compact size, the grand concert is ideal for younger and smaller guitarists. The most famous example is the size 0 Martin guitar.
(See Scale Length and Concert Guitar.)

Grunge Music [Genre]

A genre that emerged in the mid-1980s and thrived in the early 1990s. More than just a music style; grunge was also a subculture. Grunge, a blend of **rock** and **punk**, is known for its dark and dirty sounds, popularised by Seattle bands like Nirvana, following the decline of '**hair metal**'.

With its rough-around-the-edges sound, **fuzzy** guitars, and angsty lyrics, grunge wasn't just a style of music; it was an attitude that embodied the frustrations of the youth.

(See Rock and Punk Music and Hair Metal in General Slang Terms and Fuzz in Slang for Guitar Sounds.)

 Grunge Music Examples: *Bands:* Nirvana, Alice in Chains, Hole, The Smashing Pumpkins, Pearl Jam, Mudhoney.

Half Note (aka Minim, 1/2) [Rhythm]

A half note (American) or minim (British) is a type of **note value** where a single note lasts as long as half of a 4-beat **bar**. It has a time value equal to two **quarter notes**, meaning there are two beats per bar.
The musical notation symbol for a 1/2 note looks like this:
(See Note Value, Bar and Quarter Note.)

Half Step / Tone (See Semitone)

Hammer-On [Playing Technique]

When you press down a finger on a string, pick a note and then hit (hammer) another finger on the same string to produce a second note. Hammer-ons are a type of **articulation** known as '**slurs**' used mainly as a **lead guitar** technique but also to make chord work sound more vibrant.
(See Articulation, Slur and Lead Guitar.)

Harmonics [Music Theory]

Sound waves (notes) whose **frequencies** are whole number multiples of a primary note frequency, called a **fundamental**. For example, the top E string on a guitar has a fundamental frequency of 82.4Hz; the next harmonic is, therefore, 164.8Hz (82.4 x 2).
(See Frequency and Fundamental Note.)

Harmony

Harmony is when you play two or more notes at the same time. It can be used to create a sense of unity, excitement, or even sadness. We call **chords** "harmony", which are made by combining notes from scales – primarily the **major scale**. **Rhythm guitar** playing revolves around mostly playing chords and harmony.
(See Chord, Major Scale and Rhythm Guitar.)

Heavy Metal Music (See Metal Music)

Hollow-Body Guitar [Guitar Types]

An electric guitar with a hollow cavity inside its body that was created in response to the need for amplification in Big Band ensembles. Jazz guitarist Charlie Christian is credited with creating the *first electric guitar in 1936 by attaching an electronic **pickup** to his acoustic guitar. (*See **Good to know** below).

Hollow guitars have a unique **archtop** shape with an f-hole, which allows air to circulate. They're a preferred choice among blues and jazz guitarists who appreciate

their smooth, rich sound. The hollow-body guitar is known for generating unwanted **feedback** when played through loud amps, leading to the creation of **semi-hollow** variants.
(See Feedback, Archtop and Semi-Hollow Guitar and Pickups in Parts of an Electric Guitar.)

 Good to know: The first manufactured electric guitar was a lap steel guitar created in 1931 by a chap named George Beauchamp. The guitar was affectionately nicknamed the "Frying Pan".

Hook [Songwriting & Composition]

A catchy musical **phrase** that is often repeated throughout a song to grab the listener's attention and stay in their memory. For example, in the song *Sweet Child O' Mine* by Guns N' Roses, the hook is the famous guitar **riff** that opens the song and repeats throughout.
(See Phrase and Riff in General Slang Terms.)

Improvisation [Playing Technique]

When a musician plays and composes music passages, such as a **guitar solo**, off the cuff without prior preparation. Great improvisation (aka improv) requires creative expression, technical prowess, and a deep understanding of the various areas of music theory (and how to apply them).
Improving your improv skills takes time and effort, so be ready to practise regularly. Keep pushing yourself, and enjoy the journey.
(See Solo, Guitar.)

Hybrid Picking [Playing Technique]

When a guitarist uses their fingers and a **plectrum** to pick the strings. This technique allows the player to create complex patterns and **melodies** that would be difficult to achieve using just a pick or fingers alone.
(See Melody and Plectrum in Guitar Accessories Terms.)

Indie Music (aka Indie Rock) [Genre]

Also called 'alternative rock', indie is a music genre whose name refers to artists who release their music through smaller, independent record labels (e.g. Mute Records and Creation Records) instead of major corporate labels like Sony and EMI. Indie stands for 'independent charts', which was the first chart for independently signed artists in the UK, launched in 1980.

Originally, indie artists produced music in various genres, but now the term is mostly associated with a particular style of music, regardless of the record label.

 Indie Music Examples: Artists: The Smiths, Cocteau Twins, Oasis, Pixies, The Verve, Radiohead, White Stripes.

Instrumental

When we say a piece of music is an "instrumental," it means that it is played using musical instruments, like a guitar or piano, without any vocals or lyrics. Instrumentals are often used as background music for movies, TV shows, video games, and commercials. They can also be enjoyed on their own as standalone pieces of music.

Instrumentation

The process of choosing and organising the different instruments that will be used to create a musical composition.

Interval [Music Theory]

A musical unit of measurement that tells us the distance between two notes. For example, the interval between A-A♯ is one **semitone** (one fret), aka one half step or **minor third**. The interval between F-G is one **tone** (two frets), aka one whole step or **major third**.
(See Semitone, Minor Third, Tone and Major Third.)

Interval Formula (aka Interval Pattern)
[Music Theory]

A pattern of numbers representing **intervals** that tell us the notes that make up a scale, chord, or chords within a **chord progression**. For example, 1-3-5 is the formula for the interval and the corresponding notes that make a **major chord**. And 1-2-3-4-5-6-7 is the interval formula for the **major scale**.
(See Interval, Chord Progression, Major Chord and Major Scale.)

Intonation

How in tune a guitar stays across the entire fretboard length. To check if the intonation of your guitar is correct, use a guitar tuner, play an open string, and then pick the

note on the 12th fret of the same string. Both notes should show the same **pitch**.
(See Pitch.)

Inversion (See Chord Inversion)

Jazz Music [Genre]

A style of music evolved from a mixture of African and later European influences. Jazz has its cultural origins in the songs of the enslaved West African peoples forced to work on plantations in the American South in the late 1800s. Jazz focuses on virtuoso playing, advanced chord changes, **syncopated rhythms** and **improvisation**. It often fuses with various music styles and, as a result, has numerous sub-genres, such as gipsy-jazz, free-jazz and jazz-rock.
(See Syncopation, Rhythm and Improvisation.)

 Jazz Music Examples: *Guitarists:* Freddie Green, Wes Montgomery, George Benson, Emily Remler, Eric Gale, Barney Kessel.

Jazz Standard [Genre]

Popular songs and compositions, mainly from the heyday of jazz (the 1920s to 1950s) that have become part of the 'standard' jazz musicians' repertoire. If you want to learn some jazz standards on your guitar, *Autumn Leaves, Angel Eyes, Misty, Summertime,* and *Fly Me To The Moon* will keep you busy for a while.

Jumbo Guitar [Guitar Types]

The largest acoustic guitar shape you can get. With its big body, you get a big sound. Owing to the increased air inside the body cavity, a jumbo produces a deep, resonant **tone** and louder volume with slightly more **sustain** than a standard acoustic. Jumbos are similar to **dreadnought** guitars, except they have a deeper rounded body design.
(See Tone, Sustain and Dreadnought Guitar.)

Just Intonation (aka Pure Tuning) [Music Theory]

A system of tuning **intervals** based on whole number ratios related to the mathematical **overtones** musical instruments produce, such as 3:2 and 4:3. Most modern-day music uses **12-tone equal temperament** tuning.
(See Interval, Overtone and Twelve-Tone Equal Temperament.)

Key Signature (aka Key) [Music Theory] [Songwriting & Composition]

Like a recipe that tells you what ingredients to use, a key signature shows you the notes and chords that work best together. Each key signature has a unique set of **sharps** (♯) and **flats** (♭). Learn popular key signatures like C, G, D, and A major to make learning songs and **improvisation** easier.
(See Improvisation and Sharp & Flat Notes.)

Lead Break (aka Guitar Solo)

A section of a song where a guitarist plays a **guitar solo** or **improvises** over an **instrumental** passage. Lead

breaks typically showcase the guitarist's technical skills and musical creativity.
(See Solo, Guitar, Improvisation and Instrumental.)

Lead Guitar (See Solo, Guitar)

Legato [Rhythm] [Playing Technique]

A smooth and connected style of playing where notes flow seamlessly into each other without any breaks or pauses in between them.

Luthier

A skilled person who repairs, adjusts, or builds stringed instruments, such as guitars, mandolins and violins.

Major Chord [Music Theory]

A chord that is made from the 1st, 3rd and 5th notes of a **major scale**, with the **interval formula** 1-3-5. For example, the notes in the C major scale are as follows: C-D-E-F-G-A-B, so the notes in a C major chord (aka CMaj, C) are C-E-G. Major chords sound happy, upbeat and cheerful and are also known as **'triads'**.
(See Major Scale, Interval Formula and Triad.)

Major Key [Music Theory]

A **key signature** where the **harmony** (chords) and notes (**melodies**) are taken from the **major scale**. Songs written in a major key have a happy, upbeat vibe. A major key has a specific pattern of **semitones** (half steps) and **tones**

(whole steps) that determines the notes and chords that can be used. For example, the G major scale notes are G, A, B, C, D, E, and F#. The chords in the key of G major are G major, A minor, B minor, C major, D major, E minor and F# diminished.
(See Key Signature, Harmony, Melody, Major Scale, Semitone and Tone.)

Major Key Song Examples: *Don't Look Back in Anger* by Oasis | *Chocolate* by The 1975 | *Here Comes the Sun* by The Beatles | *More Than a Feeling* by Boston.

Major Scale [Music Theory]

One of the most important **diatonic scales** in music, which contains seven notes separated by a fixed pattern of **semitone** and **tone intervals.** You can see here: Tone-Tone-Semitone-Tone-Tone-Tone-Semitone.
(See Diatonic Scale, Semitone, Tone and Interval.)

Major Second, Interval [Music Theory]

A musical **interval** that is the distance between two notes separated by one **tone**, which is equal to two **semitones** or two frets. E.g. C-D. Symbol: **M2**
(See Interval, Tone and Semitone.)

Major Seventh, Interval [Music Theory]

A musical **interval** that is the distance between two notes separated by 11 **semitones**, which is equal to 11 frets. E.g. C-B. Symbol: **M7** *(See Interval and Semitone.)*

Major Sixth, Interval [Music Theory]

A musical **interval** that is the distance between two notes separated by nine **semitones**, which is equal to nine frets. E.g. C-A . Symbol: **M6**
(See Interval and Semitone.)

Major Third, Interval [Music Theory]

A musical **interval** that is the distance between two notes separated by four **semitones**, which is equal to four frets. E.g. C-E. Symbol: **M3**
(See Interval and Semitone.)

Melody (aka Melodic Line)

A sequence of single notes from a **scale** that produces a tune. When playing a **melody** on the guitar, you pluck the strings using either a guitar pick or your fingers. To make a melody more expressive, guitarists often use techniques, such as **vibrato**, **slides**, and **bends**.
(See Scale, Melody, Vibrato, Slide and Bend.)

Metal Music (aka Heavy Metal) [Genre]

First appearing in the UK in the late 1960s, heavy metal is a type of rock music characterised by loud **distorted** electric guitars, double bass drum beats, and aggressive vocals. With **shredded** guitar solos, heavy **riffs** and dark lyrical themes, heavy metal has spawned many subgenres, notably thrash, glam, and the not-so-cheery sounding death and doom metal.
(See Distortion in Slang for Guitar Sounds and Shredding and Riff in General Slang Terms.)

Metal Music Examples: *Bands:* Iron Maiden, Black Sabbath, Motörhead, Judas Priest | *Guitarists:* Zakk Wylde, John Petrucci, Vivian Campbell, Dimebag Darrell.

Meter / Metre [Rhythm]

The arrangement of recurring rhythmic patterns of **accents**, **strong beats** and **weak beats** that provide not only the **rhythm** of the music but dictates its **feel**. *(See Accents, Strong Beats, Weak Beats, Rhythm and Feel.)*

Microtonal Music [Music Theory]

Music containing **intervals** smaller than the conventional Western **semitone**, which are found in the tuning system called **twelve-tone equal temperament** (12-TET).
To explain further, a semitone (e.g. the gap between the notes F-F#) can be broken down into smaller units known as 'cents'. There are 100 cents per semitone, and micro tuning uses these tiny intervals.
(See Interval, Semitone and Twelve-Tone Equal Temperament.)

Minim (See Half Note)

Minor Chord [Music Theory]

A chord made from the 1st, flattened 3rd and 5th notes of the **natural minor scale**, with the **interval formula** 1-♭3-5. For example, the A natural minor scale notes are A-B-C-D-E-F-G, so the notes in an A minor chord (aka Amin, Am)

81

are A-C-E. Minor chords are a type of **triad** that help create a sad and sombre mood.
(See Minor Scale, Interval Formula and Triad.)

Minor Key [Music Theory]

A **key signature** where the chords and notes are based on a corresponding **minor scale**. Songs written in a minor key have a sad sound that tugs at your heartstrings.
(See Key Signature and Minor Scale.)

Minor Key Song Examples: *Heart of Gold* by Neil Young | *Titanium* by David Guetta | *Nothing Else Matters* by Metallica | *Wish You Were Here* by Pink Floyd

Minor Scale [Music Theory]

Three main types of minor scales exist; the natural minor (aka Aeolian mode), harmonic minor and melodic minor scales. The natural minor scale is a **diatonic scale** built by starting on the sixth note of its **relative major scale**. E.g. the E natural minor scale is formed when you start on the 6th note of the G major scale.
(See Diatonic Scale, Relative Major and Major Scale.)

Minor Second, Interval [Music Theory]

A musical **interval** that is the distance between two notes separated by one **semitone**, which is equal to one fret. E.g. C–Db. Symbol: **m2**
(See Interval and Semitone.)

Minor Seventh, Interval [Music Theory]

A musical **interval** that is the distance between two notes separated by ten **semitones**, which is equal to ten frets. E.g. C–Bb. Symbol: **m7**
(See Interval and Semitone.)

Minor Sixth, Interval [Music Theory]

A musical **interval** that is the distance between two notes separated by eight **semitones**, which is equal to eight frets. E.g. C–Ab. Symbol: **m6**
(See Interval and Semitone.)

Minor Third, Interval [Music Theory]

A musical **interval** that is the distance between two notes separated by three **semitones**, which is equal to three frets. E.g. C–Eb. Symbol: **m3**
(See Interval and Semitone.)

Modes [Music Theory]

A set of seven **scales** created when you start on different notes in the **major scale**. Modes can up your guitar-playing game because they give you a wider range of sounds and moods to choose from when playing **solos** and **melodic lines**. For example, the Dorian mode has a dark, mysterious sound, while the Mixolydian mode has a bright, bluesy sound.
(See Scale, Major Scale, Solo, Guitar and Melody.)

Modulation [Music Theory]

When a piece of music changes from one **key** to another, either going up or down in **pitch** to change the **tonal centre**. Modulation is like switching gears and adds interest and surprise to the music, keeping listeners engaged.
(See Key Signature, Pitch and Tonal Centre.)

Movable Chord

A collective name to describe chord shapes you can move up and down the fretboard using the same finger formation, e.g. **barre chords** and **power chords**.
(See Barre Chord and Power Chord.)

Music

Music is a pattern of sounds and silence organised using three main elements: **melody**, **harmony**, and **rhythm**. In **Western music**, all sounds you hear are created from 12 notes, which are arranged into **scales**.
(See Melody, Harmony, Scale and Western Music.)

Music Notation

A written representation of a musical composition that shows the parts for different instruments on separate lines called **staves**.
(See Stave.)

Music Score

A written record of music that tells a musician how a piece of music is to be played. Music scores consist of symbols and marks that show information such as which notes to play, their duration, **tempo**, and more. *(See Tempo and Sheet Music.)*

> **Good to know:** 'Score' and 'sheet music' are often used interchangeably, but a score is a complete manuscript with music for many instruments, while sheet music is typically used by an individual to see the music for their instrument.

Musical Alphabet [Music Theory]

A sequence of 12 note **pitches** that creates **melodies** and **harmonies** in **Western music**. Seven are natural notes (A, B, C, D, E, F and G), and five have sharp or flat signs after them (A#/Bb, C#/Db, D#/Eb, F#/Gb and G#/Ab). You can use the musical alphabet to find any note on the guitar fretboard when you know the names of the open strings. *(See Pitch, Melody, Harmony and Western Music.)*

Musical Director

Also called a 'conductor' in classical styles of music, the musical director is the person who oversees all areas of musical production and performance. They are typically responsible for auditioning musicians, overseeing rehearsals, creating musical arrangements, and more.

Natural Notes [Music Theory]

The seven notes in the **musical alphabet** that are neither sharp (#) or flat (b): A, B, C, D, E, F, and G.
(See Musical Alphabet.)

Neck Relief

The amount of curve along the length of a guitar neck, which controls the space between the fretboard and the strings (aka **string action**).
(See Action.)

Note Value (aka Rhythm Value or Subdivision) [Rhythm]

The length of time a note, chord, or **beat** rings out for. 'Subdivision' describes taking a note (beat) and breaking it down into various notes that are shorter than one beat. Examples include **1/4th**, **1/8th**, **16th** and **triplet** notes.
(See Beat, Quarter, Eighth and Sixteenth Note and Triplet.)

Octave [Music Theory]

A musical **interval** that is the distance between two notes separated by 12 **semitones**, which is equal to 12 frets. The high-**pitch** note is double the **frequency** of the low-pitch note. E.g. C-C.
(See Interval, Semitone, Pitch and Frequency.)

Octave Shape [Playing Technique]

Playing two notes an **octave** apart at the same time to create textured **melodic lines** and **licks**. Octave shapes

are used frequently by jazz, funk and rock guitarists. Listen to *Give Me The Night* by George Benson to hear an example of octave shapes in action.
(See Octave and Melody and Lick in General Slang Terms.)

Offbeat [Rhythm]

The **weak beats** that occur between the **strong beats** of a **bar**. In a 4/4 **time signature**, the offbeats occur on the "and" counts: 1 **and** 2 **and** 3 **and** 4 **and**.
(See Weak Beats, Strong Beats, Bar and Time Signature.)

Onbeat [Rhythm]

The first **beat** of each music **bar,** often called the **downbeat**. The term onbeat can also refer to every downbeat in a bar (e.g. beats 1, 2, 3 and 4 in a 4-beat bar), not just the first beat, depending on the musical context.
(See Beat, Bar, Downbeat.)

Open Chord

A chord with open strings that ring freely without being pressed (fretted). Open chords are fundamental beginner shapes played on the guitar's lower frets. You can also move them up the guitar neck and change their **pitch** using a device called a **capo**.
(See Pitch and Capo in Guitar Accessories Terms.)

Outro (aka Coda) [Songwriting & Composition]

The climactic end section of a song. An outro can be a repeat of the **chorus**, **verse** or **bridge** or a completely new passage with unique **chord progressions**, musical textures and vocals. An outro can also end with a fade-out, where the volume of the music slowly drops to zero. *(See Chorus, Verse, Bridge and Chord Progression.)*

Overtone [Music Theory]

Additional higher-pitched **frequencies** produced when you play a note on an instrument. The main note your ear detects is called the **fundamental frequency**, and overtones are the extra resonant frequencies created. *(See Fundamental Note and Frequency.)*

Palm Mute [Playing Technique]

A technique where the side of the picking hand lightly touches the strings near the guitar's **bridge** to dampen the sound. Doing this can produce a muted, percussive effect or silence the strings. Palm muting can add a **dynamic** and **rhythmic** element to music. *(See Dynamics and Rhythm and Bridge in Parts of an Electric Guitar.)*

Parlour / Parlor Guitar [Guitar Types]

A compact narrow-waisted guitar with an elongated body shape. The name comes from the small venues and parlour rooms of the 19th century in which the guitar was originally played. Today, the distinct **mid-range tone** of a parlour guitar means it's a popular choice playing **slide guitar**, **blues** and **folk music**. It's also a good travel guitar, thanks to the compact size. *(See Slide Guitar, Blues and Folk Music and Mid-Range in Slang for Guitar Sounds.)*

Passing Tone [Playing Technique]

A note that smoothly connects two other notes in a chord or **melody**. You can use techniques such as **hammer-ons, pull-offs** and **slides** to create passing tones to add some flair to your playing. They can help make the blandest chord changes sound more impressive and expressive.
(See Melody, Hammer-On, Pull-Off and Slide.)

Pentatonic Scale [Music Theory]

A musical scale with five notes used to play **solos** and **melodies** in genres such as **rock** and **blues music**. It gets its name from the Greek word 'pente', which means five, and 'tonic', which means tones. There are two types of pentatonic scales: major and minor. The major pentatonic scale is brighter and more cheerful, while the minor pentatonic scale is sadder.
(See Solo, Guitar, Melody, Rock and Blues Music.)

Perfect Fifth (Interval) [Music Theory]

A musical **interval** that is the distance between two notes separated by seven **semitones**, which is equal to seven frets. E.g. C-G . Symbol: **P5**
(See Interval and Semitone.)

Perfect Fourth (Interval) [Music Theory]

A musical **interval** that is the distance between two notes separated by five **semitones**, which is equal to five frets. E.g. C-F. Symbol: **P4** *(See Interval and Semitone.)*

Phrase [Playing Technique]

The movement of a group of notes that create a complete musical expression. Musically, the term "phrasing" refers to how you play the notes, including elements of **rhythm**, **timing**, and **feel**. A musical phrase can also be called a melodic line or **melody**.
(See Rhythm, Timing, Feel and Melody.)

Picking [Playing Technique]

Plucking individual strings with your **fingers** or a **guitar pick** to play a **melody** or notes within a chord shape.
(See Fingerstyle, Flatpicking and Melody.)

Pinched Harmonic [Playing Technique]

A **lead guitar** technique where a guitarist activates **harmonics** on the fretboard by lightly touching the string with the thumb as they pick. **Overtones** of the main note produce a distinctive sound used primarily in **metal** styles of music. To hear the sound of a pinched harmonic, listen to *Juice* by Steve Vai.
(See Lead Guitar, Harmonics, Overtone and Metal Music.)

Pitch

The perceived highness or lowness of a sound. On a guitar, the pitch is determined by the **frequency** of the vibrating string, which is influenced by factors such as string tension, length, and thickness.
(See Frequency.)

Polyrhythms [Rhythm]

African drumming traditions inspired the use of polyrhythms in music, which is when two or more **rhythms** are played at the same time to create exciting new patterns. An example of this is a guitarist playing a strumming rhythm in 4/4 **time** (**signature**) while a drummer plays a drum pattern in 3/4 time.
(See Rhythm and Time Signature.)

Pop Music [Genre]

A widely popular genre of music with commercial appeal that originated in the UK and America during the 1950s. Pop includes any music style currently popular and encompasses various sub-genres, including **folk**, **rock**, **country**, **R&B**, and EDM (electronic dance music), among others.
(See Folk, Rock, Country and Rhythm and Blues Music.)

 Pop Music Examples: *Artists:* Rihanna, Charlie Puth, Madonna, Adele, Coldplay, The Beatles, Jess Glynne.

Power Chord

Chord shapes consisting of only two notes (the **root** and **fifth**) played across two or three guitar strings. They're a staple in **rock** and **metal music**, often used for their powerful and driving sound, and are frequently played on electric guitars with **distortion** or **overdrive** effects. *(See Root Note, Perfect Fifth, Rock and Metal Music, and Distortion and Overdrive in Slang for Guitar Sounds.)*

Pre-Bend (aka Pre-Dives) [Playing Technique]

A **lead guitar** technique where a guitarist bends a note up a **semitone** or **tone** then picks the string and releases it back down to its neutral position.
(See Lead Guitar, Semitone and Tone.)

Pre-Chorus (See Bridge)

Pull-Off [Playing Technique]

When you pull your finger off a guitar string in a downward motion – instead of picking it – causing the string to vibrate and produce a sound. Pull-offs are used in both **lead guitar** and **rhythm playing** and help guitarists to play faster and create fluid **legato** phrases. They're a great way to add variety to your playing and make your solos or chords sound more advanced.
(See Lead Guitar, Rhythm Guitar and Legato.)

Punk Music (aka Punk Rock) [Genre]

If you're a fan of music that challenges authority, you might enjoy punk. This genre originated in the US during the 1960s as 'garage rock', a raw and edgy style of **rock 'n' roll**. It later evolved in the UK during the 1970s, fuelled by the era's social and economic turmoil.

Punk guitar is often **distorted** and played with fast, aggressive **power chords** to create a raw and intense sound. Characterised by high-energy performances, rebellious lyrics and short songs, the punk rock scene was rude, lewd and full of attitude.

(See Rock and Roll Music and Power Chord and Distortion in Slang for Guitar Sounds.)

 Punk Music Examples: *Artists:* Sex Pistols, The Clash, Ramones, Blondie, Buzzcocks.

Quarter Note (aka Crotchet, 1/4) [Rhythm]

A quarter note (American) or crotchet (British) is a type of **note value** where a single note lasts one quarter (one beat) of a 4-beat **bar**. It has a time value equal to two **eighth notes**, meaning there are four beats per bar. The musical notation symbol for a quarter note looks like this: *(See Note Value, Bar, Eighth Note and Music Notation.)*

♩

Ragtime Music [Genre]

With its roots in New Orleans in the 1890s, ragtime music is characterised by its innovative use of **syncopated rhythms**, which were considered groundbreaking at the time. The style's name comes from its 'ragged rhythms', which were influential in the development of early **jazz music**.

Ragtime musicians were mainly African Americans who blended elements of black spirituals (a genre of religious **folk music** borne from the struggles of slavery), military marches and **blues music**. Though ragtime was traditionally piano-based music, many blues and country guitarists have adapted the style to the guitar beautifully. *(See Syncopation, Jazz, Folk and Blues Music.)*

 Ragtime Music Examples: *Guitarists:* Big Bill Broonzy, Reverend Gary Davis, Memphis Minnie, Robert Johnson, Pink Anderson.

Refrain [Songwriting & Composition]

A short **melody**, **phrase** or lyrical line usually found at the beginning or end of a verse of a song that repeats throughout. The word refrain is Latin for the term "to repeat". The phrase repetition serves to reinforce a particular element the songwriter wants to emphasise. *(See Melody and Phrase.)*

Refret

A process of replacing the **frets** on a fretted stringed instrument such as a guitar, banjo, or ukulele. The old frets are removed, and new ones are installed to fix **intonation** issues, prevent buzzing, and improve overall playability.
(See Intonation and Frets in Parts of an Acoustic Guitar.)

Reggae Music [Genre]

A genre of music created in the late 1960s in Jamaica. Combining elements of **ska**, **R&B** and **rock**, among other styles, reggae is famous for its distinctive **offbeat rhythms**, known as 'skank'. Many consider *mento* – the traditional folk music of Jamaica – to be the roots of reggae music.

Reggae music has a deep connection to the Rastafari movement, with Bob Marley's music playing a significant role in being a voice for oppressed Afro-descendants. His messages of hope, equality, and peace resonated with many, and continue to do so today.
(See Offbeat and Ska, Rhythm and Blues and Rock Music.)

 Reggae Music Examples: *Artists:* Bob Marley and The Wailers, Culture, Lee "Scratch" Perry, Toots and the Maytals, Aswad.

Relative Major [Music Theory]

A major scale that has the same notes as its **relative minor scale**. This means that you can use the same chords and scales in both **key signatures**, which makes it easy to switch between them. To find the relative major of its relative minor on the guitar, shift three frets up from the minor key **root note**. For example, C major is the relative major of A minor.
(See Relative Minor, Key Signature and Root Note.)

Relative Minor [Music Theory]

The relative minor is like the gloomy twin of its **relative major**. Their scales and chords share the same notes, but their different starting points (**root note**) create distinct emotions. Minor sounds sad, major sounds happy. To find the relative minor on the guitar, shift three frets

down from the root note of the major. For example, A minor is the relative minor of C major.
(See Relative Major and Root Note.)

Resonance

This refers to how sound waves bounce around and amplify within a space or object. When you pluck a guitar string, the sound waves vibrate through the instrument's body and create resonance. This is what gives each note its characteristic **timbre**.
(See Timbre.)

Rhythm [Rhythm]

The pattern of sound and silence in a piece of music. Rhythm can refer to the underlying pulse and how notes and rests are organised into **phrases**. It can also refer to the particular style or **groove** of a piece of music, such as a **swing** rhythm in **jazz** or a **reggae** rhythm in pop music. Finally, rhythm can also refer to how music is physically performed, such as the rhythmic strumming or picking of a guitar or the percussive beats played on a drum kit.
(See Phrase, Swing, Jazz and Reggae Music and Groove in General Slang Terms.)

Rhythm and Blues Music (aka R&B, Soul) [Genre]

Like so many music genres, rhythm and blues (R&B) was created by black musicians who united influences of **gospel**, **blues**, **jazz** and soul. Early R&B music emerged in 1940s America with a more soulful and rootsy vibe centred around emotional singing and pulsing rhythms.

Contemporary R&B music tends to focus on electronic sounds and studio production over live instruments and songs.
(See Gospel, Blues and Jazz Music.)

 R&B Music Examples: *Classic:* Aretha Franklin, Etta James, The Isley Brothers, Ray Charles | *Contemporary:* Alicia Keys, Usher, Boyz II Men, Mary J. Blige.

Rhythm Guitar [Rhythm]

The technique of playing **chords** and providing the **harmonic** and **rhythmic** foundation for a song. Rhythm guitar is a crucial part of popular music, and it can also be a specific role in a band. In this role, a guitarist plays the rhythm parts while someone else plays the **melodies** and guitar **solos**.
(See Chord, Harmony, Rhythm, Melody and Solo, Guitar.)

Rhythm Section [Rhythm]

The section of a band responsible for providing the backbone of the music through a combination of drums, bass, and other instruments, such as guitar, piano and percussion. Their combined efforts create a cohesive and **dynamic** sound that underpins the rest of the band.
(See Dynamics.)

Rock and Roll Music (aka Rock 'n' Roll) [Genre]

A music genre created in the United States at the end of the 1940s, taking inspiration from both African-American

blues and white **country music** to create an electrifying new sound. The birth of rock 'n' roll was a testament to the power of music to transcend social and racial barriers, but it was also a reflection of the deeply ingrained racism of its time. Black performers were subjected to discriminatory laws that prevented them from sharing the stage with white performers, staying in certain hotels, and even making eye contact with white audience members.

However, teenagers of all races found common ground at the rock 'n' roll shows and refused to let hate divide them. Eventually, the Civil Rights Act paved the way for desegregation, allowing music to bring people together, regardless of skin colour.

Known for simple 3-4 chord song structures and guitar-driven instrumentation, other styles that influenced the genre included **rhythm and blues**, **jazz**, and **rockabilly**. The profound social and political significance of rock 'n' roll, along with its lasting impact on future musical genres, has solidified its place in history and in the hearts of many music lovers.
(See Blues, Country, Rhythm and Blues, Jazz and Rockabilly Music.)

 Rock 'n' Roll Music Examples: *Artists:* Little Richard, Eddie Cochran, Bill Haley and His Comets, Jerry Lee Lewis | *Guitarists:* Bo Diddley, Sister Rosetta Tharpe, Chuck Berry, Buddy Holly.

Rock Music [Genre]

A broad style of music known for amplified electric guitars, powerful drums, heavy **distortion** sounds and

edgy vocals. Rock developed as early as the 1940s, influenced chiefly by **rock 'n' roll**, **blues** and **country music**. Like other music genres, early rock music was adopted by the youth of the day as a form of expression, rebellion and escapism, with guitar playing a central element in creating its electrifying sounds.
(See Rock and Roll, Blues, and Country Music and Distortion in Slang for Guitar Sounds.)

 Rock Music Examples: *Bands:* Aerosmith, The Who, Led Zeppelin, Bon Jovi | *Guitarists:* Slash, Ritchie Blackmore, Jennifer Batten, Brian May.

Rockabilly Music [Genre]

Emerging from post-World War II America, rockabilly is a fusion of **country** and **blues** and is considered the precursor of **rock 'n' roll music**. During its golden era, Sun Records studios in Memphis was the hub of rockabilly music and produced legendary recordings for artists such as Elvis Presley and Carl Mann.

Rockabilly rhythm guitar liberally used the famed 1-4-5 (written as I-IV-V) blues **chord progression**, while the **semi-hollow guitar** and upright bass gave rockabilly its distinctive swinging 'twangy' sound. The style had a significant impact on future generations of musical styles (modern offshoots include psychobilly and punkabilly) and the history of popular music.
(See Chord Progression, Semi-Hollow Guitar and Country, Blues and Rock and Roll Music.)

Rockabilly Music Examples: *Artists:* Elvis Presley, Carl Perkins, Sonny Burgess, Warren Smith, Jerry Lee Lewis.

Root Note [Music Theory]

The first note in a **chord** or **scale** that defines its name and **key.** It is usually the lowest **pitch** note. For example, G is the root note in a G **major chord** and B is the root note in the B **minor scale**. The root note is the foundation note that supports the other notes in a chord or scale and makes them sound **harmonious**.
(See Chord, Scale, Key Signature, Pitch, Major Chord, Minor Scale and Harmony.)

Saturation

An effect that happens when an audio signal (such as from a guitar) is amplified beyond its usual limits. It involves passing the signal through an **overdriven** amplifier or **effects pedal** to produce a gritty, fuller sound, similar to mild **distortion**.
(See Overdrive and Distortion in Slang for Guitar Sounds and Effects Pedal in Guitar Accessories Terms.)

Scale

A sequence of notes separated by specific **intervals**. The two most common scales in **Western music** are the **major** and **natural minor scales**. Major scales radiate positivity and are commonly used in **pop**, **rock**, and **country** genres, while minor scales add depth and emotion to **blues**, **jazz**, and **classical music**.

Scales are also a powerful tool for mastering the fretboard and enhancing your guitar skills.
(See Interval, Western Music, Major Scale, Minor Scale and Pop, Rock, Country, Blues, Jazz and Classical Music.)

Scale Length

The distance between the vibrating part of a guitar string between the **nut** and **saddle**. Guitar makers use other measurements, with the average scale length of **a full-size guitar** between 24.75 and 25.5 inches.
(See Full-Size Guitar and Nut and Saddle in Parts of an Acoustic Guitar.)

Semi-Hollow Guitar [Guitar Types]

An electric guitar that has a partial hollow cavity inside the body and a wooden centre block where the **pickups** are mounted to prevent **feedback**. Often with iconic f-hole sound holes that aren't just for looks but to allow air to flow, these guitars are popular with blues, jazz and blues-rock guitarists who love their warm acoustic **tone**. An example of a popular semi-hollow guitar is the Gibson ES-335, played by blues icon B.B. King.
(See Feedback, Tone [Sound] and Pickups in Parts of an Electric Guitar.)

Semitone (aka Half Step & Half Tone) [Music Theory]

The **interval** between one note and its neighbouring note. On the guitar, this is the distance between one fret and the fret next to it. For example, the distance between notes C-C♯.
(See Interval.)

Setup

A maintenance procedure where various adjustments are made to a guitar to ensure optimum playability and sound. Typically carried out by a skilled **luthier** or technician, a setup can include tweaks to the guitar's **action**, **neck relief** and **intonation**.
(See Luthier, Action, Neck Relief and Intonation.)

Seventh Chord [Music Theory]

A colourful-sounding chord built from four notes, which are popular in styles such as **jazz, bebop,** and **funk music**. Think of it like a **triad** chord with an extra note added on that's either an **interval** of a **major seventh** or a **minor seventh**.
(See Jazz, Bebop and Funk Music, Triad, Interval, Major and Minor Seventh.)

Sharp (#) & Flat Notes (♭) [Music Theory]

Alterations to the **pitch** of a musical note. A sharp raises the pitch of a note by one **semitone** (aka half step), while a flat lowers the pitch by one semitone. For example, A# is one semitone higher in pitch than A, while A♭ is one semitone lower in pitch than A.
(See Pitch and Semitone.)

Sheet Music

A written or printed document that displays the **musical notation** of a song, which can include **melody, harmony, rhythm,** and other instrumental parts for musicians to read and perform.

(See Music Notation, Melody, Harmony and Rhythm.)

Sixteenth Note (aka Semiquaver, 1/16th) [Rhythm]

A sixteenth note (American) or semiquaver (British) is a type of **note value** where a single note lasts as long as one-sixteenth of a 4-beat **bar** (a quarter of a beat). It has a time value equal to half an **eighth note**, meaning there are 16 sixteenth beats per bar. The **musical notation** symbol for a 1/16th note looks like this:
(See Note Value, Bar, Eighth Note and Music Notation.)

Ska Music [Genre]

Originating in Jamaica in the mid-20th century, ska is a genre of music with an upbeat party vibe characterised by **offbeat rhythms**, pacy **tempos** and iconic fashion style. Heavily influenced by Jamaican **folk music** (namely mento and calypso), ska also mixes **jazz** and **R&B** and is considered the ancestor of **reggae** and the subgenre known as 'two tone' music.
(See Offbeat, Tempo and Folk, Jazz, Rhythm and Blues and Reggae Music.)

Ska Music Examples: *Artists:* Prince Buster, The Specials, Madness, The Skatalites, The Ethiopians.

Slide [Playing Technique]

When you play a note with your fretting hand and slide the finger to another fret without lifting it off. This technique creates a smooth and flowing transition between two notes.

Slide Guitar [Playing Technique]

A technique where a musician uses a small metal or glass tube to glide over the guitar strings. This creates a unique sound that's often used in **blues** and **country music**. The slide allows the player to produce smooth **glissando** notes.
(See Blues and Country Music and Glissando.)

Slur [Playing Technique]

A sign in musical notation that tells the musician to play a passage of two or more notes in a flowing **legato** style, that is to say, without pauses between the notes. Different types of slurs are more commonly known to the hobby guitarist as **hammer-ons**, **pull-offs** and **trills**. *(See Legato, Hammer-On, Pull-Off and Trill.)*

Solid-Body Guitar [Guitar Types]

A guitar designed without any **sound holes** – unlike an acoustic guitar – to eliminate **feedback** when played through an amplifier. The solid-body guitar is the most popular type of electric guitar and is made from a solid piece of wood, or various types of wood joined together.

With 21-24 frets on average, Gibson and Fender are the two most famous brands of solid-body electric guitars.
(See Feedback and Sound Hole in Parts of an Acoustic Guitar.)

Solo, Guitar (aka Lead Break) [Playing Technique]

A **melodic** passage played on the guitar over a song section or as a complete musical arrangement. Guitar solos feature **improvisation**, the proficient use of **scales** and various lead guitar techniques, such as **hammer-ons**, **vibrato** and **bends**. Musicians perform solos in virtually all genres of music, from **classical** to **blues** to **jazz**.
(See Melody, Improvisation, Scale, Hammer-On, Vibrato, Bend, Classical, Blues and Jazz Music.)

Staccato [Rhythm] [Playing Technique]

A playing technique where each note is played short and detached from the next, creating a stabbing and percussive effect.

Standard Guitar (See Full-Size Guitar)

Standard Tuning

The most common tuning method used for six-string guitars, which are tuned from low to high: E, A, D, G, B, E. The open strings are tuned to three consecutive **perfect-fourth intervals** (E to A, A to D, and D to G), followed by a **major third** interval between G and B, and finally, another perfect-fourth interval between the B and top E strings.
(See Interval, Perfect Fourth and Major Third.)

Stave (aka Staff)

Also called a 'staff', a stave is a series of five horizontal lines used to write **music notation**. The lines are numbered from bottom to top, with the bottom line being number one. Notes are placed on the lines and spaces between the lines to indicate their **pitch**.
(See Music Notation and Pitch.)

String Gauge

The thickness of a guitar string. The thicker the string, the lower the **pitch**. Different string gauges are used for different styles of music. For example, thicker strings are often used in styles of music like **metal music**, where guitarists sometimes detune their strings to play in alternative tunings (e.g. **drop d tuning**). On the other hand, thinner strings are often used for playing styles such as **jazz music**.
(See Pitch, Drop D Tuning, and Metal and Jazz Music.)

String Skipping [Playing Technique]

When a guitarist skips over one or more strings while playing a sequence of notes, such as a **scale**. This helps improve coordination and accuracy and allows you to make creative **melodic** runs from scales instead of just going up and down them. String skipping requires precise picking and **fretting** hand coordination, as well as good **muting** skills to avoid unwanted noise.
(See Melody, Scale, Fretting and Palm Mute.)

Strong Beats [Rhythm]

Beats in a **bar** that drive the pulse stronger than others. Taking **4/4 timing** as an example, the first **beat** in a bar has the strongest **accent**, whilst beat 3 is the second strongest. Beats 1 and 3 are thereby called strong beats. *(See Bar, Time Signature, Beat and Accents.)*

Strumming Pattern [Playing Technique]

A repeated sequence of upstrums and downstrums in a sweeping motion played across multiple guitar strings with a plastic **plectrum** (aka guitar pick) or the fingers. A guitarist typically strums chord shapes. *(See Plectrum in Guitar Accessories Terms.)*

Sustain

The length of time a note continues to ring out after it has been played. A guitar with "good sustain" will allow the notes to ring out longer.

Sweep Picking [Playing Technique]

A picking technique where the guitarist picks consecutive notes in the same direction. For instance, up/up/up/up or down/down/down/down.

Swing Music [Genre]

An offshoot of **jazz music** which emerged in the United States in the late 1920s, swing got its name from the 'swinging' rhythms of the Big Band musicians who performed this style of music. Swing was hugely popular throughout the 1930s and 1940s and became a staple at dance halls, owing to its use of **offbeat syncopation** and **triplet** note grooves.

Swing rhythm guitar has a relaxed vibe, with two distinct styles; a swing feel, where the downstrokes are played longer than the upstrokes, and a straight feel characterised by snappy **quarter note** strums.
(See Jazz Music, Offbeat, Syncopation, Triplet and Quarter Note.)

 Swing Music Examples: *Artists:* Duke Ellington, Glenn Miller, Ella Fitzgerald, Michael Bublé, | *Guitarists:* Freddie Green, Mike Bryan, Mary Osborne, Django Reinhardt.

Syncopation [Rhythm]

A **rhythmic** technique in music where the emphasis is placed on ordinarily **unaccented beats**. For example, in music arranged into a pattern of four beats per **bar**, such as **4/4 timing**, the **onbeats** are felt as the **strong beats**. So accenting the **weak beats** or **offbeats** creates a syncopated feel.
(See Rhythm, Accents, Beat, Bar, Time Signature, Onbeat, Strong Beats, Weak Beats and Offbeat.)

Tablature (aka TAB)

A guitar-specific form of **music notation** with numbers and symbols that help guitar players learn songs and techniques. Commonly known as 'TAB', it shows the

placement of fingers on a guitar's fretboard rather than the traditional staff notation used in **sheet music**.
(See Music Notation and Sheet Music.)

Tag [Songwriting & Composition]

A type of **bridge** that connects two sections of a song. Generally, just a few **bars** long, a tag is primarily used when the last lyrical line of a **chorus** hangs over into the **verse**, thus connecting the two sections.
(See Bridge, Bar, Chorus and Verse).

Tapping [Playing Technique]

When a player uses their fingers to tap on the strings of a guitar or stringed instrument to create sounds without plucking or strumming them. Tapping allows the musician to play fast, complex **melodies** and **solos**. It is often used in genres such as **metal** and **rock**, where speed and precision can be desirable.
(See Melody, Solo, Guitar, Metal and Rock Music.)

Tempo [Rhythm]

The speed we play notes and chords in a piece of music. Tempo is typically measured in beats per minute (BPM).

Through-Composed [Songwriting & Composition]

Unlike song structures with repeated sections (such as a **verse**, **chorus** or **bridge**), through-composed music has a continuous, ever-changing flow. That is to say, each section appears only once and is never to be heard from again. To hear an example of a through-composed pop

song, listen to *The Musical Box* by Genesis.
(See Verse, Chorus and Bridge.)

 Through-Composed Song Examples: *In Dreams* by Roy Orbison | *Bohemian Rhapsody* by Queen | *Happiness is a Warm Gun* by The Beatles

Timbre (aka Tone Quality) [Rhythm]

The unique quality of a sound often described as the 'colour' of a sound. Timbre is what distinguishes one instrument or voice from another. For example, a guitar's timbre differs from that of a piano or saxophone.

Time Signature [Rhythm]

A musical measurement that tells you how many **beats** there are in each **bar** and what type of **note value** it is. The most common time signatures in music are 2/4, 3/4, 4/4, and 2/2. 4/4 timing indicates there are four **quarter note** beats in each bar, and 3/4 tells you there are three quarter notes per bar.
(See Beat, Bar, Note Value, and Quarter Note.)

Timing [Rhythm]

A musician's ability to play in sync with the **rhythm** and **beat** of a song. In guitar playing, good timing means playing the notes and chords in the right **tempo**, while playing with a sense of **groove** and **feel**.
(See Rhythm, Beat, Tempo, Feel and Groove in General Slang Terms.)

Tonal Centre (aka Tonality) [Music Theory]

The way the notes or **pitches** of a piece of music are organised and related to each other. Tonality establishes a **key** centre, with the **tonic** being the most important note in that key, around which the other notes are organised.
(See Pitch, Key Signature and Tonic.)

Good to know: 'Tonic' and 'tonal centre' are often used interchangeably but differ subtly. The 'tonic' is the first note and chord of a scale that provides stability and resolution. 'Tonal centre' is a broader term that can refer to any note or chord that defines the tonality of music, which may or may not be the same as the tonic, and can also change throughout a piece. (You may need to read that last bit over a few times until it clicks!)

Tone (aka Whole Step) [Music Theory]

A term with multipurpose meanings in music; in this first of four definitions, 'tone' refers to the **interval** or distance between two notes with one note separating them. This is the interval between two frets on the guitar. For example, the distance between notes C-D.
(See Interval.)

Tone (Frequency)

Here, 'tone' refers to a single pure sound wave defined by a particular **frequency** measured in Hertz (Hz). An example of tone used in conversation: "I can hear a high-

pitched *tone* coming from the speaker; it must be the audio engineer listening to a test *tone*."
(See Frequency.)

Tone (Note) [Music Theory]

A word used by musicians to mean a musical note. An example used in conversation: "You're playing a G, but I'm pretty sure it's a different *tone*; try G sharp or A."

Tone (Sound)

A word music lovers use to refer to the unique sound quality of a sound source. An example used in conversation: "My new maple wood acoustic guitar produces a beautiful warm *tone*."

Tonewood [Guitar Types]

A particular type of wood used in making guitars. Some tonewoods are rarer and more expensive, like Brazilian rosewood or mahogany, which are highly valued for their rich **tone**. However, because of concerns about the environment and ethics, guitar makers are now searching for alternative tonewoods that are sustainable and eco-friendly. Some tonewood examples that are kinder to the planet include cedar, spruce and sapele.
*(See Tone [Sound] and **Alternative & Sustainable Guitar Woods** near the end of the book.)*

Tonic [Music Theory]

Also known as the 'home note', the tonic is the first note or **degree** of a **scale** or **key signature**. It typically starts and ends a piece of music, and the chord built on the tonic is the main focus of a song. It sounds stable and serves as the natural resting place in a piece. For example, in the key of D major, the note D is the tonic note and the D major **triad** is the tonic chord.
(See Degree, Scale, Key Signature and Triad.)

Transpose [Music Theory]

To change the key of a piece of music. Specifically, it means the process by which notes in a **melody** or **chord** are shifted up or down in **pitch**. Transposition is often done to suit the vocal range of a singer or the specific capabilities of an instrument.
(See Melody, Chord and Pitch.)

Tremolo [Playing Technique]

A rapid up-and-down variation in the volume of a note or chord. Tremolo is created using techniques like wiggling a **tremolo arm** on an electric guitar, repeatedly plucking strings, or using an **effects pedal**.
(See Tremolo Arm in Additional Guitar Parts Terms and Effects Pedal in Guitar Accessories Terms.)

Triad [Music Theory]

A chord that contains three notes arranged in a specific pattern of skipping every other note. For example, a C

major triad contains the notes C-E-G, with a **major third interval** between C and E, and a **minor third** interval between E and G. The four types of triads are **major, minor, diminished**, and **augmented**.
(See Interval, Major Third, Minor Third and Major, Minor, Diminished and Augmented Chord.)

Trill [Playing Technique]

A combination of **lead guitar** techniques known as 'slurs', where you play multiple **hammer-ons** and **pull-offs** in succession. Trills help you play rapid, repeated notes that are faster than picking each note individually with a guitar pick.
(See Lead Guitar, Slur, Hammer-On and Pull-Off.)

Triplet [Rhythm]

A group of three notes played within the duration of two notes of the same value. For example, three triplet **quarter notes** would be played as long as two regular quarter notes. Guitarists often use triplets in their **solos** and **riffs** to create complex and **dynamic rhythms**.
(See Quarter Note, Solo, Guitar, Dynamics, Rhythm and Riff in General Slang Terms.)

Tritone (Interval) [Music Theory]

A **dissonant** sounding musical **interval** that is the distance between two notes separated by six **semitones**, which is equal to six frets. E.g. C-F♯ (aka augmented 4th) or C-G♭ (aka diminished 5th).
(See Dissonance, Interval and Semitone.)

Good to know: The tritone, also known as 'diabolus in musica' (devil in music), was condemned in early Western music because of its dissonant, unsettling quality. The Catholic Church even banned it during the Middle Ages due to its devilish sound. But hey, what's music without a little rebellious dissonance, right? Rock on, tritone!

Turnaround [Songwriting & Composition]

A brief **instrumental** interlude that occurs at the end of a musical section. The typical turnaround **chord progression** transitions the song back to a previous passage, such as a **verse** or **chorus**.
(See Instrumental, Chord Progression, Verse and Chorus.)

Twelve-Tone Equal Temperament [Music Theory]

The standard modern musical tuning system used in **Western music**, in which the **octave** is divided into 12 equal **semitones**.
(See Western Music, Octave and Semitone.)

Unison Bend [Playing Technique]

A string **bending** technique where two notes are played simultaneously used widely by blues and rock guitarists, to name a few. To play a unison bend, you pick a note on one string, then pick and bend an adjacent string up to the same **pitch**. To hear an example of unison bends, listen to the intro **riff** on *Highway Chile* by Jimi Hendrix.
(See Bend, Pitch and Riff in General Slang Terms.)

Upbeat [Rhythm]

Traditionally, an upbeat is the last beat in a **bar**. However, the definition varies between musical genres; in **classical orchestral music**, the term "upbeat" refers to the upward stroke of the conductor's arm. Many musicians also use the phrase to describe the "ands" between the bar's **downbeats**, as shown in bold here:
1 **and** 2 **and** 3 **and** 4 **and**.
(See Bar, Downbeat and Classical Music.)

Verse [Songwriting & Composition]

A song section that sets up the story or message of the song. It often has a different **melody** and **chord progression** from the **chorus** and is usually repeated throughout the song. A verse often builds anticipation for the catchy sing-along chorus.
(See Melody, Chord Progression and Chorus.)

Vibrato [Playing Technique]

A technique used mainly in **lead guitar** playing, where you press a finger on a string and play multiple **bends** to alter the note's **pitch**. Vibrato is an expressive technique guitarists of all styles use to add dimension and spirit to their playing. Using a **tremolo arm** or **vibrato effects pedal** also recreates a vibrato effect.
(See Lead Guitar, Pitch, Bend and Tremolo Arm in Additional Guitar Parts Terms and Effects Pedal, Vibrato in Guitar Accessories Terms.)

Walking Bass Line

A bass melody where a continuous series of **quarter notes** (a beat per bar) helps to outline the underlying **chord progression** of a song via the use of **scales** and **arpeggios**. The effect of a walking bass line is to move the **rhythmic** motion of the music forward. You can hear instances of this playing style mainly in **swing**, **jazz**, and **blues music**.
(See Quarter Note, Chord Progression, Scale, Arpeggio, Rhythm and Swing, Jazz and Blues Music.)

Weak Beats [Rhythm]

The weaker **accents** in a **bar** of music. For instance, in **4/4 timing**, beats 1 and 3 are emphasised and are known as the '**strong beats**'. Beats 2 and 4 are not as stressed and are labelled as the weak beats.
(See Accents, Bar, Time Signature and Strong Beats.)

Western Music

A broad term that encompasses various musical styles that originated or developed in Europe and its colonies, such as North America. Some examples of Western music genres are **rock**, **country**, **funk**, **jazz** and **blues**.
(See Rock, Country, Funk, Jazz and Blues Music.)

Whole Note (aka Semibreve) [Rhythm]

A whole note (American) or semibreve (British) is a type of **note value** where a single note lasts the duration of an entire 4-**beat bar**. It has a time value equal to four

quarter notes, meaning one beat per bar. The musical notation symbol for a whole note looks like this:
(See Note Value, Beat, Bar and Quarter Note.)

Whole Step (See Tone)

PART THREE

GUITAR & MUSIC SLANG TERMS

Guitar & Music Slang Terms

This section will cover some of the most common guitar-related slang terms that can confuse newcomers. Some are so well-known they've become ingrained in popular culture.

It's helpful to know that the use of slang terms by guitarists is widespread and can vary greatly depending on factors such as location and genre. This means that a pedal steel player from Birmingham, Alabama might use different lingo than a rock guitarist from Birmingham, UK.

Let's delve into the world of guitar slang, and don't worry, we'll skip the inappropriate ones. More tea, vicar?

Slang for Guitar Sounds

" ───────

Check out this **dirty** guitar **fuzz** sound, it's proper **meaty**.

─────── "

If you're new to playing guitar, terms such as "distortion", "crunch," and "fuzz" might leave you scratching your head. To add to the confusion, these words can have different meanings depending on who you ask. This section clears things up for you.

Good to know: We often use the words 'EQ', 'tone' and 'saturation' when describing guitar sounds. Look them up in *Glossary of Guitar Terms* for definitions.

Clean

An electric guitar sound free of **distortion** or **overdrive** effects, resulting in a pure, clear tone that closely resembles the guitar's natural sound. To get a clean sound, lower the amplifier **gain** and increase the master volume to avoid overdriving the amp.
(See Distortion, Overdrive and Gain.)

Clean Sound Song Examples: *Give Me The Night* by George Benson | *Under The Bridge* by Red Hot Chilli Peppers | *Sultans of Swing* by Dire Straits

Crisp (aka Bright)

A "crisp" guitar tone has a clear and bright sound with balanced **low**, **mid**, and **high frequencies**. This type of sound is well-defined and favoured by many music enthusiasts. The opposite of a crisp tone is usually described as being "**muddy**" or "dull".
(See Low-End, Mid-Range, High-End and Muddy.)

Crunch (aka Crunchy)

An electric guitar sound midway between **clean** and **distorted** that's usually associated with **rhythm guitar** sounds in genres such as classic **rock**. When an amplifier has a moderate amount of **gain**, you get a tone described as "crunchy", which is synonymous with a "gritty" or "**dirty**" sound.

From chords to **riffs** and **melodies**, adding some crunch to your amp adds flavour and bite to your playing without the face-melting gusto of distortion.
(See Clean, Distortion, Gain and Dirty and Rhythm Guitar, Melody and Rock Music in Glossary of Guitar Terms and Riff in General Slang Terms.)

Crunch Sound Song Examples: *You Shook Me All Night Long* by AC/DC | *All Right Now* by Free | *Pride and Joy* by Stevie Ray Vaughan

Good to know: Guitar tone also depends on how you set the amplifier and the guitar's volume and EQ controls.

Dirty

There are different ways to describe the sound of a **distorted** guitar, and "dirty" is one of them. It's the opposite of a **clean** guitar sound and is achieved by cranking up the **gain** control on an amplifier (usually between 6-10). A popular sound used in many genres, particularly **rock**, **punk** and **metal**, you can also get a dirty tone by using guitar **effects pedals**.
(See Distortion, Clean and Gain and Rock, Punk and Metal Music in Glossary of Guitar Terms and Effects Pedal in Guitar Accessories Terms.)

 Dirty Sound Song Examples: *No One Knows* by Queens of the Stone Age | *American Idiot* by Green Day | *War Pigs* by Black Sabbath

Distortion

The deliberate alteration of a guitar's sound to create a distorted, rough, or edgy tone. This effect is achieved by intentionally overloading the amplifier or using a **distortion pedal**. Distortion is a key element in **rock**, **metal**, alternative, and experimental music. It creates diverse tones that range from aggressive and powerful to lo-fi and gritty.
(See Rock and Metal Music in Glossary of Guitar Terms and Effects Pedal, Distortion in Guitar Accessories Terms.)

 Distortion Sound Song Examples: *My Wave* by Soundgarden | *Paradise City* by Guns 'n' Roses | *Don't Stop Me Now* by Queen

Fuzz (aka Fuzzy)

Fuzz is an alternative word for "**distortion**", "**dirty**", and "**overdrive**" when describing a guitar sound. The distinctive 'fuzzy' sound results from a saturated guitar signal that's typically produced by a **fuzz effects pedal**. Think of a really annoyed swarm of bees caught in a jar before flying away to freedom, and you're in the ballpark of the fuzz sound.
(See Distortion, Dirty and Overdrive and Effects Pedal, Fuzz in Guitar Accessories Terms.)

 Fuzz Sound Song Examples: *Comfortably Numb* by Pink Floyd | *Plug in Baby* by Muse| *Crosstown Traffic* by Jimi Hendrix

Gain

A measurement of how much an amplifier's **pre-amp** section amplifies an electric guitar signal. The higher the gain, the higher the level of **distortion** or saturation in the sound.
(See Distortion and Pre-Amp in Guitar Accessories Terms.)

High-End (aka Top-End or Treble)

An **EQ** term that refers to the highest end of the **frequency** spectrum of a sound we can hear. The range is between 4kHz (4,000 Hz) and 7kHz (7,000 Hz). Balanced high-end will make a guitar sound **crisp** and bright; too much and the tone will be thin and harsh.
(See Crisp and EQ and Frequency in Glossary of Guitar Terms.)

Good to know: The audible range of human hearing is 20Hz to 20,000Hz, but as we age, our high-frequency hearing drops to around 15,000Hz to 17,000Hz. That's part of life. So, you could say, "I'm not getting old, I'm just getting more selective about what I listen to!"

Jangly (aka Jangle or Twangy)

A jangly guitar sound is usually produced by an electric guitar with lots of treble **EQ**. The jangly sound is primarily heard on strummed **open chord** shapes in **pop**, **indie** and **folk music genres**. Many bands from the 1960s and 1980s are famous for their jingly-jangly guitar tones.
(See EQ and Pop, Indie and Folk Music in Glossary of Guitar Terms.)

Jangly Sound Song Examples: *There She Goes* by The La's | *Turn! Turn! Turn!* by The Byrds | *This Charming Man* by The Smiths

Low-End (aka Bottom-End or Bass)

An **EQ** (equalisation) term that refers to the low end of the **frequency** spectrum of a sound that lies around 20Hz to 250Hz. Low-end frequencies are further divided into sub-bass (around 20Hz to 60Hz) and bass (around 60Hz to 250Hz). A balanced low-end will make a guitar sound warm and rich; too much and the sound is muddy and muffled.
(See EQ and Frequency in Glossary of Guitar Terms.)

Meaty (aka Beefy, Fat or Full)

When someone says a sound is "meaty", they're talking about an instrument or music mix sound with generous **low** and **mid-range frequencies** that pack a substantial punch. Similar words used for this type of full-bodied sound are "chunky", "deep", and "thick".
(See Low-End and Mid-Range and Frequency in Glossary of Guitar Terms.)

 Example of "meaty" in use:

> "I love the meaty tone analogue tube amps produce."

Mid-Range (aka Mids)

An **EQ** term that refers to a broad range of **frequencies** in the middle of the frequency spectrum of a sound we can hear. Mid-range lies approximately 300 to 4kHz (4,000 Hz). Balanced mids will make a guitar sound clear and **clean**, too much will be boxy, and too little can make it sound dull and lifeless.
(See Clean and EQ and Frequency in Glossary of Guitar Terms.)

Middle 8 (See Pre-Chorus in Glossary of Guitar Terms)

Muddy

A word used to describe a sound which lacks clarity and even balance of **treble**, **middle** and **bass frequencies**.

The culprits for a muddy guitar sound can be too much bass **EQ**, old strings and poor playing technique, all of which cause a lack of definition and **crispness.**
(See Crisp, High-End, Mid-Range, Low-End and EQ and Frequency in Glossary of Guitar Terms.)

 Example of "muddy" in use:

> "Turn up the treble on your guitar, man; it sounds muffled and muddy."

Overdrive

A saturated guitar sound similar to, but less extreme than, **gain** and **distortion.** Overdrive was originally created by cranking up the dials on a valve tube amplifier, thus clipping (overdriving) the signal. You add a gritty overdriven sound to a guitar via an amplifier or **overdrive effects pedal.**
(See Gain and Distortion and Effects Pedal, Overdrive in Guitar Accessories Terms.)

 Overdrive Sound Song Examples: *Where The Streets Have No Name* by U2 | *Johnny B. Goode* by Chuck Berry | *Basket Case* by Green Day

Warm (aka Mellow)

A warm sound has boosted **low-end** and **mid-range** frequencies and subtle **high-end** frequencies. A "warm" **tone** can refer to the mellow character of the wood a guitar is made from or the **pickup** and amplifier settings. **Semi-hollow guitars,** used chiefly in **blues** and **jazz music**, are known for their warm, rich sound.

(See Low-End, Mid-Range and High-End and Pickups in Parts of an Electric Guitar and Tone [Sound], Semi-Hollow Guitar and Blues and Jazz Music in Glossary of Guitar Terms.)

General Slang Terms

> " ———
>
> I took my **jazz box** for a **jam** and
> made sure not to **fluff** anything.
>
> ——— "

Air Guitar

A high-energy performance where you mimic playing a guitar with outrageous moves, electrifying air solos, and headbanging to your favourite tunes. Air guitar is all about rocking out with pure imagination.

Axe / Ax [Guitar Types]

Another name for a guitar. The origins of the term "axe" dates back to the 1950s when jazz musicians used it as slang for the saxophone and other popular jazz instruments. As with many slang terms, guitarists soon adopted the word and continue to use it to refer to a guitar today.

 Good to know: The name "axe" is typically slang for an electric guitar but can also apply to an acoustic or bass guitar.

Backline

A term used in live performance that refers to the audio equipment and gear a band needs to perform at shows. The equipment typically includes amps, speakers, drum risers, guitar cables and more.

Behind the Beat [Rhythm]

This phrase is related to **rhythm** and **timing**. Music is arranged into **beats** and **bars**. To play "behind the beat" (aka to **groove**) means to play along with a piece of music, **metronome** or other musicians with natural, relaxed timing. In opposition, if you play "ahead of the beat" it means you're rushing.
(See Groove and Rhythm and Timing, Beat and Bar in Glossary of Guitar Terms and Metronome in Guitar Accessories Terms.)

 Example of "behind the beat" in use:

> "You're speeding up when you play along with the backing track. Slow down and play behind the beat."

Cans

A word used to refer to over-ear headphones, so-called because the ear cups resemble large cans.

 Example of "cans" in use:

> "I prefer using cans when recording guitar because they block out more outside noise."

Chicken Picking / Pickin' [Playing Technique]

The technique of **hybrid picking** the guitar strings to produce a percussive sound in **country-style music** circles. But why is it called "chicken picking"? I can almost hear you ask. The **staccato** sound the technique produces on the guitar strings is said to sound like a chicken clucking. I'm not making it up. Do an internet search and listen for yourself.

(See Hybrid Picking, Country Music and Staccato in Glossary of Guitar Terms.)

Chops [Playing Technique]

If another musician asks to hear some of your chops, they're not being personal; they want you to show off your repertoire of playing skills. The origins of the word are rooted in **jazz music** when it was used to describe a brass-instrument player with the superior ability to easily hit tricky notes. Given this, having "great chops" suggests you play with remarkable **technique**, **feel** and **timing**. Chops away!

(See Jazz Music, Good Technique, Feel and Timing in Glossary of Guitar Terms.)

 Example of "chops" in use:

> "He's got some mad jazz chops." (Referring to a guitarist who plays jazz-style guitar proficiently.)

Fluff (aka Fluffed Up)

One of many words musicians use to describe when you make a mistake on an instrument. Other vibrant synonyms for a musical mess-up include "botch", "goof" and "fumble". This is a very catchy term, so don't be surprised if you say it yourself next time you make a boo-boo on guitar.

 Example of "fluffed" in use:

> "I need to play the melody line again. I fluffed up the first few notes."

GAS

This acronym stands for 'guitar acquisition syndrome' and labels a person obsessed with buying lots of musical gear. The phrase was coined by Walter Becker of the band Steely Dan in a magazine article in the 1990s and is now a worn-out burn (insult) used by folk lurking about on online forums.

Gitfiddle [Guitar Types]

If you find yourself in the deep south of America, a guitarist may call their guitar (or other type of stringed instrument) a "gitfiddle". The term originally comes from combining the words "git" (shortened version of the word "guitar") plus "fiddle".

Groove [Rhythm]

A sense of musical flow that propels a song forward. When a musician talks about "getting in the groove" or "feeling the groove", it means they're locked into the **rhythm** and **feel** of the music and are playing in sync with the music or other musicians.

A groove can vary in intensity and complexity depending on the genre and mood of the music.
(See Rhythm and Feel in Glossary of Guitar Terms.)

Guitar Face

A comical or exaggerated facial expression a guitarist makes when playing a guitar **solo** or **melody**. These facial gestures range from intense concentration (aka "tongue-poking-out-look") to pained grimaces. The burning question is - do *you* have a guitar face?
(See Solo, Guitar and Melody in Glossary of Guitar Terms.)

Guitar Tech

Short for guitar technician, this person is part of the crew (aka **backline** techs) and they maintain, repair and **set up** guitars and basses for a band while they're on the road.
(See Backline in General Slang Terms and Setup in Glossary of Guitar Terms.)

Hair Metal (aka Glam Metal) [Genre]

A derisive term used to describe a branch of heavy **metal music** of the 1980s. The phrase pokes fun at the heavy metal musician stereotype who wore long, big '80s hair' and flamboyant glam clothing. Hair metal was characterised by loud **distorted** guitars and overtly sexual lyrics the modern listener may call "cheesy", with a good dose of over-the-top stage theatrics. Bands that have earned their "hair metal badge" include Whitesnake, Def Leppard and Poison.
(See Metal Music in Glossary of Guitar Terms and Distortion in Slang for Guitar Sounds.)

Hook [Songwriting & Composition]

The catchiest and most memorable part of a song. This could be anything from the vocal melody, a guitar **riff**, a piano **melody** or a percussive **rhythm** that stays in the listener's head.
(See Riff and Melody and Rhythm in Glossary of Guitar Terms.)

Jamming (aka "to Jam") [Playing Technique]

A freeform **improvisation** on your instrument where you can express yourself, play with different techniques and styles, and enjoy the freedom of creating music on the fly. You can jam alone, with a backing track or hook up with other players and have a blast.
(See Improvisation in Glossary of Guitar Terms.)

 Example of "jamming" in use:

"I took my guitar to Gabriel's place and we were jamming for a few hours."

Jazz Box [Guitar Types]

Slang for a **semi-hollow** body guitar, which is also called an '**archtop guitar**'. As you'd expect from the name, these guitars are most commonly used by jazz guitar players, but they're also a favourite of many blues and rock players due to their distinctive warm **tone**.
(See Semi-Hollow, Archtop Guitar and Tone [Sound] in Glossary of Guitar Terms.)

Les Paul [Guitar Types]

A shortened version of the Gibson Les Paul, a type of electric guitar designed by Gibson in the 1950s. Named after renowned guitarist and innovator Les Paul, many rock and metal guitarists love the guitar, as it is known for its rich **meaty tone** and **sustain.**
(See Meaty in Slang for Guitar Sounds and Sustain in Glossary of Guitar Terms.)

Lick [Playing Technique]

A quick musical **phrase** played on the guitar that adds flair to a tune. A lick is similar to a **riff** and can also be thoughts of as a mini slice of a **guitar solo**. It's also a way to practise your **chops** and show off your skills.
(See Riff and Chops and Phrase and Solo, Guitar in Glossary of Guitar Terms.)

Noodling [Playing Technique]

When your fingers take a musical stroll on the guitar, producing impromptu **melodies** or **riffs** without much thought or structure. Noodling is a guilty pleasure for guitarists, sometimes annoying for others nearby during band rehearsal breaks! Noodling at home can be fun to experiment with sounds and ideas, but don't overdo it. Structured practise yields the best results.
(See Riff and Melody in Glossary of Guitar Terms.)

Riff [Playing Technique]

A pattern or series of notes that form a memorable and distinctive musical **phrase.** Riffs are associated with music genres such as **rock**, **blues**, and **metal**. Listen to the start of the song *Smoke on The Water* by Deep Purple or *Seven Nation Army* by The White Stripes for examples of two classic guitar riffs in action.
(See Phrase and Rock, Blues and Metal Music in Glossary of Guitar Terms.)

Shredding (aka "to Shred") [Playing Technique]

When a skilled guitarist plays complex, fast **lead guitar**, they're said to be "shredding". This style involves the use of numerous musical scales and techniques, such as **alternate picking**, **sweep picking**, and **finger tapping**. The term originates from the idea that playing so fast and ferocious could literally "shred" your fingers or guitar fretboard to pieces. Smokin' hot!
(See Lead Guitar, Alternate Picking and Sweep Picking and Tapping in Glossary of Guitar Terms.)

Six String (aka 6-String) [Guitar Types]

A guitar with six strings. Listen to the opening line of the song *Summer of '69* by Brian Adams: "I got my first real six-string", he sings, meaning he got his first guitar.

Slash Chord

A chord with a different note in the low bass position other than its **root note**. The term comes from the fact a

slash symbol appears in the chord name, e.g. C/G (pronounced "C slash G" or "C over G"), which is a C **major chord** with a G note in the bass position.
(See Root Note and Major Chord in Glossary of Guitar Terms.)

Strat [Guitar Types]

A shortened version of the Fender Stratocaster, a type of electric guitar designed by Leo Fender and produced by Fender Musical Instruments. Strats have a distinctive **double-cutaway** shape, three **single-coil pickups**, and a **vibrato tremolo system**. They're known for their bright, clear tone and versatile sound.
(See Cutaway, Single-Coil Pickup and Tremolo Arm in Additional Guitar Parts Terms.)

Take it From the Top

To play a passage of music from the beginning of the song or song section.

Example of "take it from the top" in use:

> The guitarist says to her band members in the rehearsal room: "Let's take it from the top of the chorus again, lads."

Tele [Guitar Types]

A shortened version of the Fender Telecaster, a **solid-body** electric guitar known for its bright, **jangly** sound and versatility across genres. It typically has two **single-coil pickups**.

(See Solid-Body Guitar in Glossary of Guitar Terms, Jangly in Slang for Guitar Sounds and Single-Coil Pickup in Additional Guitar Parts Terms.)

The Engine Room

This saying refers to the rhythm section of a band, specifically the drums and bass. They provide the energy and drive for the band's overall sound, like the engine of a vehicle powering its movement.

Tight [Rhythm]

A term that means you can play an instrument skilfully with good **timing**, **rhythm** and **feel**. It also means you can play in sync with song recordings and other musicians, creating a cohesive sound. A 'tight' band is one that sounds professional and polished.
(See Timing, Rhythm and Feel in Glossary of Guitar Terms.)

 Example of "tight" in use:

> "That rhythm guitarist is tight; they play in perfect time with the drummer and never miss a beat."

Vamp

To repeatedly play a section of music, usually just one or two chords. Vamping is often used to create a **groove** or a mood for a song, and to give space for **improvisation** or **jamming** ideas over.

(See Groove and Jamming and Improvisation in Glossary of Guitar Terms.)

Whammy Bar (See Tremolo Arm in Additional Guitar Parts Terms)

PART FOUR

GUITAR ACCESSORIES TERMS

Guitar Accessories Terms

In this closing section of the book, you'll learn the name and functions of the most popular accessories guitar players use. And as you and I both know, nobody loves an excuse to buy a bit of new gear more than a guitarist.

Amplifier

An amplifier (aka amp) is an electronic device that boosts and modifies the sound signal from a **pickup** on an electric, electro-acoustic, or bass guitar, enabling the instrument to be played at higher volumes.
(See Pickups in Parts of an Electric Guitar.)

Amplifier, Combo

Short for 'combination', this is a type of amp that combines the speakers and amplifiers in one compact unit, making them easier to transport for guitarists on the go. Two well-known examples of combo amps are the Vox AC30 and Fender Blues Junior.

Amplifier, Stack

Primarily for on-stage use, a stack amplifier consists of an amp head connected to one or more speaker cabinets (aka cabs). Stacks are more versatile and powerful than a combo amp because you can choose different heads and cabinets to suit your sound and style.

Some famous examples include the Marshall Super Lead Plexi with a 4x12 cabinet, and the Mesa Boogie Mark V with a 2x12 cabinet.

Audio Interface

A digital device that connects a guitar, microphone, keyboard and other audio sources to a computer so you can record into music software. Want to level up your guitar playing and spark some inspiration? Get an audio interface. You can record, listen, and improve your performances. It's also a valuable tool for unleashing your creative potential.

Capo

A device that changes the **pitch** of guitar notes by clamping onto the fretboard. It makes it easier to play pieces in various **keys** and **tunings**. Because some songs require a capo to match the original recording that used one, a capo is a top accessory to have.
(See Pitch, Key Signature and Standard Tuning in Glossary of Guitar Terms.)

DAW

Standing for 'digital audio workstation', a DAW is a piece of software used to record, edit and produce music, and other digital audio material. Examples of popular DAWs include Logic Pro, Pro Tools, Ableton, and Garage Band.

De-Humidifier

A device usually placed inside a guitar case or in the guitar's sound hole that absorbs excess moisture in the air. Doing this prevents swelling, warping, and cracking. If you live in a humid area or store your guitar in a damp place (above 50%), a de-humidifier can help protect your guitar from moisture-related issues.

Effects Pedal / Unit

An electronic device that changes the sound of an audio source, such as a guitar, by altering the incoming signal to produce specific effects. Effects pedals are powered by digital or analogue circuitry, and they're also called 'stomp boxes' and 'FX pedals'. Popular guitar effects pedals include **delay**, **distortion**, and **vibrato pedals**.
(See Effects Pedal, Delay, Distortion, and Vibrato.)

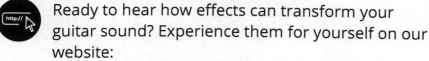
Listen to the following 14 Effects:
Ready to hear how effects can transform your guitar sound? Experience them for yourself on our website:
www.YourGuitarBrain.com/guitar-effects-pedals-audio

Effects Pedal, Chorus

An effect pedal that adds a doubled and slightly delayed copy of the guitar signal to create a thicker, richer sound. The delayed signal is also detuned somewhat to create a subtle **pitch** variation that produces a distinctive shimmering, watery sound.
(See Pitch in Glossary of Guitar Terms.)

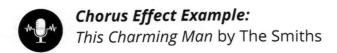

Chorus Effect Example:
This Charming Man by The Smiths

Effects Pedal, Compressor

A guitar effects pedal that reduces the dynamic range of the input signal, making the loud parts quieter and the quiet parts louder. Compressors can even out the guitar's volume and **sustain** notes longer.
(See Sustain in Glossary of Guitar Terms.)

Compressor Effect Example: *Long Train Running* by The Doobie Brothers

Effects Pedal, Delay

A guitar effects pedal that creates an echo effect by repeating the original sound after a short delay. Delay can create exciting **rhythmic** patterns and add depth to a guitar sound.
(See Rhythm in Glossary of Guitar Terms.)

Delay Effect Example:
Brighton Rock by Queen

Effects Pedal, Distortion

A guitar pedal that creates a **distorted** sound by increasing the amplitude of the guitar signal and adding **harmonic** content.

(See Distortion in Slang for Guitar Sounds and Harmonics in Glossary of Guitar Terms.)

 Distortion Effect Example:
Smells Like Teen Spirit by Nirvana

Effects Pedal, Flanger

An effect pedal that creates a jet-like whooshing sound by modulating a delayed copy of the guitar signal and mixing it with the original.

 Flanger Effect Example:
Spirit of Radio by Rush

Effects Pedal, Fuzz

A type of audio effect that alters the signal from an electric guitar to produce a **distorted**, **fuzzy** sound, often associated with **rock, indie** and psychedelic music.
(See Distortion and Fuzz in Slang for Guitar Sounds and Rock and Indie Music in Glossary of Guitar Terms.)

 Fuzz Effect Example:
Cherub Rock by Smashing Pumpkins

Effects Pedal, Loop

Also called a 'looper pedal', this effects unit enables the musician to record and loop a section of music, creating a layered and repeating sound that can be used for practise, performance, or composition.

 Loop Effect Example:
You Need Me, I Don't Need You by Ed Sheeran

Effects Pedal, Multi-Effects

A single digital effects unit that includes various types of guitar effects, such as **distortion**, **delay** and **chorus**. It allows guitarists to switch between different effects with the press of a button rather than using multiple individual effects pedal units.
(See Effects Pedal, Distortion, Delay, and Chorus.)

Effects Pedal, Overdrive

An effects pedal that boosts the **gain** of a guitar's signal to create a natural-sounding **overdrive**, similar to a **distortion** effect.
(See Gain, Overdrive and Distortion in Slang for Guitar Sounds.)

 Overdrive Effect Example:
Surfing with the Alien by Joe Satriani

Effects Pedal, Phaser

A guitar effects pedal that creates a sweeping, swirling sound by splitting the guitar signal, phase-shifting one part, and mixing it back with the original.

Phaser Effect Example:
That Lady by The Isley Brothers

Effects Pedal, Reverb

An effect created when sound waves from any sound source bounce off surfaces in a space or room. You can also recreate the reverb effect with a guitar amp or software plugin.

 Reverb Effect Example:
Hallelujah by Jeff Buckley

Effects Pedal, Tremolo

A guitar effects pedal that modulates the volume of the guitar signal, creating a wavy pulsing effect.

 Tremolo Effect Example:
Gimme Shelter by The Rolling Stones

Effects Pedal, Vibrato

A guitar effects pedal that can be used to create a "wobbling" sound effect by rapidly changing the **pitch** of the guitar's input signal. It can be used to make notes or chords sound more expressive.
(See Pitch in Glossary of Guitar Terms.)

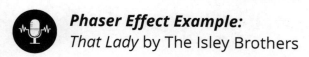 ***Vibrato Effect Example:***
Blackhole Sun by Soundgarden

Effects Pedal, Wah-Wah

A guitar pedal that allows the player to vary the tone and **frequency** response of the electric guitar signal by rocking a foot pedal back and forth.
(See Frequency in Glossary of Guitar Terms.)

 ***Wah-Wah Effect Example:***
Voodoo Chile by Jimi Hendrix

Explore all 14 effects sounds for yourself on our website. Which one tempts you?

Finger Picks

Plastic or metal picks that fit over a guitarist's fingertips, allowing them to pick individual strings and play with greater precision and speed.

Footstool (aka Foot Stand)

A short adjustable stand with a platform for a guitarist to rest their foot. The purpose is to raise your leg to help improve your playing posture.

FX Pedal (See Effects Pedal)

Humidifier

An accessory that helps maintain the proper humidity levels in a guitar's environment, preventing the instrument from drying out and potentially cracking or warping. And nobody wants that do they?

Metronome

A device that produces a regular, steady **beat** to help a musician play in time and maintain **rhythm**. The two main types of metronomes are mechanical and digital. Feel like your rhythm game is weak? Use a metronome! It'll help you improve your timing, sound more polished, and give you extra confidence.
(See Beat and Rhythm in Glossary of Guitar Terms.)

Pedalboard

A board or case that holds a guitar player's **effects pedals** and power supply in one place for easy setup and transport. Pedalboards help you protect your pedals and keep them organised.
(See Effects Pedal.)

Plectrum (aka Guitar Pick)

A small piece of plastic, wood or metal used to pick or strum guitar strings.

Pre-Amp

A device used to amplify the signal from a guitar's **pickups** before it reaches an amplifier.
(See Pickups in Parts of an Electric Guitar.)

Slide

A cylindrical tube made of glass, metal, or ceramic worn over a guitarist's fretting hand finger. When playing **slide guitar**, the slide is moved up and down the strings to create a unique sliding sound.
(See Slide Guitar in Glossary of Guitar Terms.)

Stomp Box (See Effects Pedal)

Strap, Guitar

A long piece of material attached to the body of the guitar that supports its weight while playing. They come in different materials, including leather and vegan options, such as cork and nylon for those who prefer not to use animal products.

String Winder

A device with a swivel head and handle that fits over the **tuning pegs** of a guitar so you can unwind the strings when changing them.
(See Tuning Pegs in Parts of an Acoustic Guitar.)

Tuner, Guitar

A tool that helps you tune the strings on your guitar to the correct **pitch** by measuring the **frequency** of the vibrating strings. The standard frequency for modern music is 440Hz. Guitar tuners can come in electronic or analogue versions.

(See Pitch and Frequency in Glossary of Guitar Terms.)

Alternative & Sustainable Guitar Woods

Planet Earth's resources won't last forever, and deforestation caused by greedy human activity, such as agricultural expansion and logging, means her resources are being drained. In fact, an estimated 15 billion trees are cut down each year; it's time for us to say enough is enough and do our bit.

Luckily, some guitar-manufacturing brands have become more environmentally conscious by using wood harvested responsibly to make guitars. This helps to protect endangered tree species – some of which are hundreds of years old – and promotes the long-term health of our planet.

Best Alternative or Sustainable Woods

A wood is sustainable if it comes from trees that grow quickly, don't cause much pollution when they die, or are already dead or planted for guitar making.

And guess what? Guitars made from these woods not only help protect the planet, but they can also sound gorgeous. Check out this list of eco-friendly woods that guitar makers are using these days to choose from:

- Ash
- Basswood
- Black Cherry
- Black Walnut
- Koa
- Poplar
- Red Alder
- Redwood
- Sapele
- Sitka Spruce
- Western Red Cedar
- Recyclable materials, such as oil drums, metal and cigar boxes. Look at that for creativity!

Sources:
www.impactful.ninja
www.usgreentechnology.com
www.theguardian.com
www.martinguitar.com
www.ncbi.nlm.nih.gov

THANK YOU!

If you learned something from the book, please could you spare 2 minutes to leave a review on Amazon? How did the book help your guitar journey? Did you learn any new terms? Or anything else!

Your feedback is greatly appreciated; it helps others decide and supports the author.

If you want to leave a review, head over to this book's Amazon page, scroll down, and click "Write a customer review".

Or

Scan the QR code to go straight to the Amazon review page.

QR Code Instructions:

- Open your phone's camera app
- Point at the QR code (camera will auto recognise)
- Tap the link or follow the on-screen instructions
- Go to Amazon review page. Simple!

Printed in Great Britain
by Amazon

29666736R00086